PRESIDENTIAL PERKS GONE ROYAL

Your Taxes Are Being Used For **OBAMA'S** Re-election

by political insider
ROBERT KEITH GRAY

Published by New Voices Press

315 W. 70th Street Suite 6C

New York, NY 10023

Send feedback to info@katzcreative.com

ISBN: 978-0-9748103-5-5

An application to register this book for cataloguing has been submitted to the Library of Congress.

1. Politics and Current Events 2. Political Process
3. United States Politics and Government 4. Electoral Process

Significant discounts for bulk sales are available.
Please contact indib2000@aol.com
Or call 212-580-8833

Disclaimer & Legal Notices

This book begins and ends
with this
Dedication
to
The unified voices of
concerned Americans:
Our nation's most powerful
weapon for positive change

PRESIDENT OBAMA TO DIANE SAWYER, January 25, 2010

"I'd rather be a really good one-term president than a mediocre two-term president... There's a tendency in Washington to think that our job description, the job description of elected officials, is to get re-elected."

We have noticed that tendency, Mr. President.

Table of Contents

A Troubling Time in Our History

As proud citizens of the United States of America, we insist our presidents be as protected, as fully secure from harm, as humanly possible.

This is imperative.

They are the leaders of our land and we want them to have unusual creature comforts.

They are well deserved.

They deplane on foreign lands in a luxurious display of the world's most comfortable, sophisticated and technically-advanced aircraft.

That makes us proud.

To take over many of the presidential duties, and to assist them in their campaigns for re-election, we have given our presidents freedom to enlist hundreds of "assistant presidents" with questionable qualifications, answerable only to them.

That gives us pause!

In their bargain use of presidential perks, we have given sitting presidents unfair financial advantages over competitors for their office, a threat to the democratic process.

This gives us concern.

And it should!

> *"We need to remind President Obama that we elected a president that serves beneath the law and did not anoint a king that is above the law."*
>
> —Statement from Arizona Governor Jan Brewer on August 18, 2011

CHAPTER ONE

Our Presidency Has Gone Royal

As a political science major, I have lived a charmed life. I was only thirty when I served as Appointments Secretary to United States President Dwight D. Eisenhower. In Ike's second term, he made me a member of his cabinet. In the succeeding decades, I became friend and advisor to four other of our presidents. For Ronald Reagan, I was National Communications Director during his successful campaign for the presidency. Then he made me his first presidential appointee when he named me Co-Chairman of his Inaugural. Later, I created the field of "Public Affairs" on Capitol Hill and continued to enjoy an insider's view not only of the presidential residence but, importantly, of the growing presidential perks and their negative impact on the electoral process.

From these vantage points, as the decades have passed, I began to note a very troubling trend with a compounding growth, one that now is spiraling out of control. To verify my observations, I meticulously scrutinized everything I personally saw, heard and researched. To help put together all the pieces of a highly complex puzzle and ensure that everything you read is as accurate as we could make it (and faced with some obvious camouflaging of data), I engaged professional research assistants who triple-checked or relentlessly searched for every figure and fact used in this book. A recent, former presidential chief of staff provided further assistance.

The sad but undeniable conclusion: the presidency has become a de facto principality—right under the noses of an unaware public.

Today's interested citizens rant about the Congress. They know

1

those 535 Congresspersons and Senators have their own health insurance, retirement system and repeatedly vote themselves pay raises. But behind the screens of the fully necessary security requirements, hidden under the covers of other departmental budgets, intermixed with defense spending, the escalating costs of the presidency have eluded the focus of the press or the attention of the public.

This book was not written as a partisan attack against President Obama. It began over our alarm at the spiraling number and power of the presidential perks and their assault on democracy's imperative of fair elections. President Obama is the obvious focus as the reigning president, but he particularly draws our fire as the costs of his presidency continue into the stratosphere. As the nation's economy and employment levels suffer, the numbers and costs of President Obama's supporting staff climb higher and higher. For every other expenditure in government, there is a watchdog committee, a reporting requirement and checks and balances. But no such single source or oversight exists for the expenses of the presidency. This book asks, "Why?" It also raises the question: Given the great power we give our presidents, why do we not see that their use of public funds for their re-elections is a threat to the democracy?

In the interests of full disclosure, I am in favor of less government and more individual freedom, just as our forefathers decreed when they drafted the Constitution and the Bill of Rights. Whether or not you agree with that, I ask you to keep an open mind as you read. I believe I am an intelligent, balanced observer who has grown increasingly incensed over the years—on a bipartisan basis and with good reason—by the uncontrolled and unregulated abuse of presidential privilege to the tune of billions of taxpayer dollars. Knowing the facts as I present them to you in this book, I think it will be difficult, if not impossible, for anyone to deny that these over-the-top, wildly-expensive perks have grown to the point where they severely compromise the elective process by giving the incumbent both blatant and subliminal advantages for his re-election.

There have been grumblings in the popular press about abuse of taxpayer funds. We are all understandably preoccupied to varying degrees with government spending, which has left us with a huge and still escalating national debt. However, with a new presidential election looming, the time has come for us to put a laser focus on the American presidency figuratively, "going royal." Why? Because this very expensive development does not just leach billions from taxpayer coffers, but even more dangerously, today it represents an assault on the democratic process.

Our nation's founders initially proposed calling George Washington "King George." Washington rejected that title as inappropriate for a nation based on the principle that all men are created equal. Other self-effacing and frugal presidents followed Washington. Herbert Hoover refused a presidential salary. Equally principled Howard Taft paid for the first White House automobile from his own funds. When Harry Truman left the White House, he drove his wife home to Missouri in the family car—without escort.

In the following decades, our presidents have taken on—or in many cases, taken for granted—an ever-increasing and always more dazzling array of comforts, conveniences, professional cronies, travel luxuries and other lifestyle enhancements. While we have a right to be proud when our Chief Executive arrives on foreign soil in grand style, we should at the same time be aware of and concerned about the skyrocketing variety and costs of the entire spectrum of presidential perks. Their total, in the eight years of the George W. Bush presidency, set historic records. That extravagant record was then considerably topped in only the first three years of the Obama administration.

It is a frightening trend. Non-King George Washington would be shocked and dismayed to see the many ways in which democracy's presidency has been given the job assists and lifestyle embellishments historically reserved for royals. Last year, it cost the British taxpayers $57.8 million to maintain Britain's royal family. During that same year, it cost American taxpayers some $1.4 billion to house and serve the Obamas in the White House, along with their families, friends and visiting campaign contributors.

In 2010, a year of record unemployment, when most Americans were grateful just to have a job, it was reported that 74% of White

House employees were given an average 9% raise.

Many of the costs of the presidency are hidden in the budgets of the Interior Department and its Park Service and the Defense Department as well as in legislation passed by the Congress. Ferreting out the costs of presidential perks is so challenging a task that one suspects this difficulty is deliberate.

In 2008, two months before his election to the presidency, then Senator Obama was interviewed for a piece in *Reader's Digest*. To his interviewer he said, "I passed a bill last year that sets up a searchable website where you can find every dollar of federal spending."

The bill was S.2590, but candidate Obama's statement needs some editing. First, no Senator "passes" a bill, of course. That takes a majority vote of all members of the Senate. And S.2590 was not even Mr. Obama's bill. It was Senator Coburn's bill, co-sponsored by Senator Obama along with 27 other members of the Senate, including Mr. Obama's opponent for the presidency, Senator John Mc-Cain.

But even those discrepancies would be forgiven by someone trying to arrive at an accurate summation of the presidential perks if it provided any assistance to the near-impossible job of trying to put accurate figures on the costs of perks provided by the taxpayer to our president and to the first family. Instead of giving us a search engine to explore "every dollar of federal spending," it gives us a tool to examine the many contracts our government makes with outside vendors. It will lead you to information about our government's contracts with Boeing, but it reveals little about the costs of the presidential perks. Thus, despite our best efforts at unearthing the correct figures, if any inaccurate statement or number remains in this book at the time of its printing, I suggest that it can be attributed to the deliberate obfuscation of data.

If any inaccurate figure has been used or any incorrect statement about any person appears in this book, it is both unintentional and despite our very best and very determined efforts to present the facts. And I invite you to search for the facts to see if you can find any figures more accurate than those we have used, following our research and backed by the work of our professional research assistants.

Nearing Two Billion Reasons Why We Should Care

As taxpaying citizens, it is appropriate, even urgent, that we question some items when a single year's value of presidential perks is climbing towards TWO BILLION DOLLARS! In a government supposedly bristling with checks and balances, ought we to be understandably concerned there is not a single government watchdog over total presidential expenditures?

Do you believe that any president, Republican or Democrat, needs 25 limousines reserved for him and his family; or a total of 35 helicopters, with 28 more on order? And does the president of a democracy really need dozens of jet aircraft in the presidential fleet, with their expenses hidden in Defense and Air Force budgets? Has anyone ever questioned why these numbers are so enormous, and what use is actually made of all these duplicate limos, airplanes and helicopters?

When the president makes a trip on Air Force One, he needs to ask no one for approval to make any of his very frequent trips vacationing or campaigning. When President Obama took his wife to New York for a "date night," the cost to taxpayers was several million dollars. But no force other than his conscience could have stopped him.

When the United States' billion-dollar air armada is being used politically, is it fair to taxpayers that we only be reimbursed by the president's campaign committee for the value of one first-class-commercial ticket for each passenger who is deemed aboard "for political purposes?" And is that bargain-price advantage fair to those opposing an incumbent president?

Do we think the Secretary of Defense is going to object when several hundred members of the military for whom the Secretary is accountable are used for domestic chores to serve the president's family, campaign contributors and guests at Camp David? These personnel are paid for by taxpayers and will continue to add to taxpayer expense in terms of their recruitment, payroll and retirement.

Where is our level of alarm when our president names 43 "czars" without senatorial advice and consent, and without the approval or even oversight by any other person or body? The czars are department heads or advisors personally selected and appointed by the president, at his discretion. When appointed, some of their salaries exceeded those of our elected members of Congress. These appointees have executive authority, big budgets, offices, staffs, limousines and power in various functions and regions of the country.

Why is there a need for Homeland Security Czar John Brennan when we already have Cabinet Officer Janet Napolitano, who is Secretary of Homeland Security? She runs an entire department with a $35.5 billion budget and 165,000 employees. Why then does President Obama need a czar in this area, appointed by him, reporting only to him and not confirmed by the Senate?

That's just one example of a frightening development that has only grown: the number of these appointed czars, circumventing the confirmation process or examination by any other body, has grown from 8 in President Clinton's administration to 28 during George Bush's eight years, and to 43 in the first 20 months of the Obama presidency.

President Obama has appointed 469 very senior staffers to positions that rightfully could be called "assistant presidents," 226 of them paid over $100,000 a year and 77 of them paid as much as $172,000 a year. Not one of them was voted into office or subject to the approval of any other governmental body or official.

Between his dozens of czars and hundreds of very senior staff, this president has a shadow government picked without any approval from his people or their representatives and reporting only to him. In our democracy? Sounds more like the trappings of a monarchy or dictatorship.

Should we not be concerned that no one in government is empowered—or brave enough—to tell a president it is nothing short of extravagant foolishness to have twenty-six cabin crew members for Air Force One, and FIVE chefs! Or, as it has been reported, to pay

$102,000 a year to the man who walks the first-family's dog! With his billion-dollar lifestyle, can we reasonably expect a president to identify with the real-world problems of his citizens, tens of millions of them currently unemployed?

Most troubling of all, the majority of the over-the-top extravagances and presidential prerogatives now give grossly unfair advantages to any president standing for re-election. If you favor an opposing candidate and would wish him (or her) to have a fair chance, or, if you favor President Obama but cherish fair and honest elections as an imperative basic for our democracy, does this not disturb you?

Where is our vaunted checks and balances system? I want to know, and so should you.

I am not alone in what some believe is a quixotic attempt to shed light on this shadowy but hugely significant aspect of our government and the way it works, or ,more accurately, *fails* to work properly on our behalf. I was cheered not long ago when Judicial Watch, a watchdog organization dedicated to investigating and fighting government corruption, filed a lawsuit against the Federal Government over its refusal to disclose how much we taxpayers were forced to spend, without our knowledge or consent, to send First Lady Michelle Obama, her mother, daughters, niece and nephew on an all-expenses-paid safari in Africa—a trip which was definitely in the multimillion-dollar range.

In our rough recession, isn't it high time we question whether we can afford—or truly want—a presidency gone royal? There is much we can do to turn this situation around for the good of our democracy, and I offer suggestions for doing just that in my final chapter, by which time I am betting that you will be as incensed as I am.

Still with me? Good. Then, buckle up, turn the pages, and get ready for a shock-filled ride.

"Many of these 'czars' are unconfirmed by the Senate and are largely unaccountable to Congress. Further, their activities are often outside the reach of the Freedom of Information Act (FOIA), creating a veil of secrecy about their precise role in the administration."

—David Freddoso in *Washington Examiner,* October 10, 2011

CHAPTER TWO

———◆•▪•◆———

Overkill: 43 Czars and 469 Assistant Presidents

On March 31, 2008, then Senator Barack Obama said, "The biggest problem that we're facing right now has to do with George Bush trying to bring more and more power into the executive branch and not go through Congress at all. And that's what I intend to reverse when I'm President of the United States."

What happened with this promise when he took office? President Obama has made a virtual end-run around the legislative branch. Not only are his 43 "czars" unaccountable to the Congress, but also, if subpoenaed by Congress, the President's czars can refuse to appear by claiming executive privilege, often working outside coverage of the Freedom of Information Act.

Only 8 czars in Bill Clinton's eight years. 28 czars at the end of George W. Bush' eight years. 43 czars by the end of Barack Obama's FIRST YEAR! Russia's Romanov Dynasty only produced 18 czars over 300 years!

It is most troubling that many of the czars are in competition with the assigned responsibilities of Congressional committees and with other departments of government. In most cases, they duplicate the assigned responsibilities of other officials of high rank. Some of the czars have even expanded their reach to justify their existence.

And there are some czars who might have been denied their posts had their names and backgrounds been submitted for Congressional approval. For example, John Holdren, one of the czars, has been charged as being a population-control zealot who believes

9

the Constitution justifies compulsory abortions on a massive worldwide scale. Van Jones, originally named Environmental Czar, is believed by some to be an avowed communist and anarchist.

Despite a "deal" President Obama made with Republican members of Congress when he agreed to the deficit reduction, he continues to command the services of his forty-three "czars." And, the number of the presidential czars continues to increase. The president is said to be considering the addition of a Zoning Czar, a Student Loan Czar, a Voter List Czar, a Radio-Internet Fairness Czar, a Mortgage Czar, a Land-use Czar and an Income Redistribution Czar.

This is serious business, readers, and bears repetition. Cabinet officers are picked by the president, but they must be confirmed by the Senate; their departments are funded by Congress, and they can be called before Congress to testify. The czars have been appointed by Obama at his sole discretion, are answerable only to him and, if subpoenaed by Congress, they can claim executive privilege.

This is important: the czars constitute a shadow government serving at the total pleasure of the president, answerable only to him. A government over which the people and their representatives have no control? In our treasured democracy? Sounds dangerously close to the government of a king of an eastern country or Venezuela's Chavez.

Following is the long list of czars named by President Obama:

Afghanistan/Pakistan Czar

Auto Recovery Czar

AIDS Czar

Bailout Czar

Border Czar

Car Czar

Cyber Security Czar

Copyright Czar

Climate Czar

Central Region Czar

Disinformation Czar

Domestic Violence Women Czar

Drug Czar

Education Czar

Economy Czar

Energy and Environment Czar

Export Czar

Government Performance Czar

Faith-based Czar

Health Czar

Health Insurance Czar

Homeland Security Czar

Great Lakes Czar

Green Jobs Czar

Guantanamo Closure Czar

Information Czar

Intelligence Czar

Labor Czar

Middle East Peace Czar

Pay Czar

Regulatory Czar

Safe Schools Czar

Science Czar

Stimulus Accountability Czar

Sudan Czar

TARP Czar

Technology Czar

Terrorism Czar

Tobacco Czar

Urban Czar

War Czar

Water Czar

Weapons Czar

Weapons of Mass Destruction Czar

Our government has thrived all these years without czars reporting exclusively to the president. Why now? Why so many? No wonder President Obama seems to have had a disconnect with the Congress. As we said before, he is running a shadow government of his own, one answerable only to him.

It is not as if the president is without other personal assistance. In addition to his czars, President Obama has a record-breaking 469 men and women on the White House staff with titles and salaries that qualify them for the term, "Assistant Presidents." That number of 469 does not include secretaries or junior assistants; these are titled professionals. Twenty-seven of the "Assistant Presidents," are paid over $170,000 a year; and 226 are paid over $100,000 a year. Since that is more than members of Congress were receiving until 2009, and since members of Congress have no say over President Obama's assistant presidents or czars, Congress did what Congress knows how to do best and increased its own pay to $174,000. Whammo! The taxpayers got hit, again.

None of the above is presented as denial of the enormity of presidential responsibility. It is indeed enormous. A dramatic example is the "football," the metal case that travels with the president at all times and is the ultimate trigger for nuclear warfare. An Army Lt. Colonel, a Navy Commander or a Marine Major, with the "football" handcuffed to his or her wrist, is never more than a few feet from the president.

Inside the "football" briefcase, in addition to what is known as the "Gold Codes," is a secure satellite radio along with the President's "Decision Book," a 75-page document detailing his nuclear strike options. Each morning the National Security Agency issues a new set of codes, which presidents traditionally store in their pockets—although one president once left the day's nuclear code in the pocket of a suit that went to the cleaners!

This ever-present 45-pound briefcase, containing the secret codes that allow a president to respond to a military threat with nuclear weapons, is a constant reminder that our president is Commander in Chief of the Armed Forces, both at home and around the world. In addition to that heady responsibility, he shapes the national priority, sets the national mood, and speaks for us in relationships with other nations. No question about it, his is a very responsible job.

The general public believes that the president is continuously exhausted and ever ready for the next crisis, with his every second booked to the max and little or no personal time. Nothing could be further from the truth. The late historian Milton Plesur was quoted in a 1998 book, *The Mortal Presidency: Illness and Anguish in the White House* by Robert E. Gilbert: "No responsible union would ever approve the President's hours for a 'hard hat.'" With all due respect, when he implies a president's work hours are onerous, I would argue that Plesur bought into and was perpetuating a myth that has been kept alive by writers who never worked in the White House. Any staff member who has ever worked for a president will agree that a subtle part of his or her job was to position the boss as the most overworked man in America—thus making the presidency appear to be as overwhelmingly consuming as the public believes it to be.

But consider this: if the presidency were so totally consuming, how could presidents always find the time, over many weeks, even months, to devote to campaigning for re-election? More specifically, how could President Obama find time for so many days of vacation (plus weekends) and afternoons for golf, as he did last year?

Physically, the hardest thing about the presidency is running for the job. Thanks to the saturation coverage the media gives to campaigns, the side of the presidency that the public most fully sees is the effort it takes to be elected to the post. The public assumes elected presidents continue to be as totally stressed as they were as candidates, only now, on an even higher level while involved in loftier projects.

In reality, the president is supported by total backup in every conceivable arena. Every member of the cabinet reports exclusively to the president, exists to do his bidding, is responsible for informing him on important departmental issues and, like everyone else who works closely with him, is obliged to make the president look good. These individuals must also stand ready to take the blame away from the president if anything goes amiss.

The big man has hundreds of high-priced, highly-skilled assistants committed to executing tireless performances in his name. In fact, our current Commander-in-Chief has a staggering total of more than five hundred professionals at his beck and call, all of whom work long hours and seven-day weeks to perform functions attributed to the president, to keep him on top of his job (or make him appear to be so) and, in too many cases, to help him get re-elected.

Looking Good on TV...

Thanks to his television appearances, which are run and rerun with great frequency, today's citizens see the president's job as one of continuous speechmaking. Since public speaking is a common fear among adults, people feel for a president who must be on the podium often, with the entire world watching.

While the President does make a great many public speeches, keep in mind that he does have a full-time speechwriting staff of several of the nation's best writers. The president also is supported in his public addresses by half a dozen technicians trained at servicing and operating his teleprompter. Today a presidential speech is less a speech and more a presidential reading of words drafted for him. Press conference teleprompters allow staffers to flash the president answers or statistics to make his performances appear fact-filled and flawless.

Somehow, thanks to all these helping heads and minds, there is always time for the president to receive the Thanksgiving turkey, be pictured with a Boy Scout troop or a winning ball team, to opine on a national holiday or news event, to make a political appearance, or even make surprise guest appearances on such TV talk shows as Oprah and Late Night with David Letterman. He also manages the time to campaign for himself or an ally, or take a vacation to Martha's Vineyard or even to Camp David "on unofficial business."

As Appointments Secretary for Dwight David Eisenhower, I was keeper of the presidential calendar and watcher of the clock. What I observed often reminded me that presidents are human. There are days when everything from family matters to global affairs do not go smoothly. Presidents are subject to headaches, upset stomachs and days of the blahs just like the rest of us. When Eisenhower, one of the most placid of humans, was in a rare dark mood, his valet, Mooney, would lay out a brown suit for him. It was a signal to those in the know to back off a bit and give him some space.

The media is allowed access to the presidential office and to the man himself. Presidents are so often in the news that we assume they are always terribly busy, and members of the press strengthen this belief by referring to the presidency as "life in a fishbowl." Again, far from the truth. For many days, occasionally several consecutive ones, presidents are totally out of the public eye, with no public reporting of their actions or their whereabouts. Proof that presidents are quite often out of the public's sight is the fact that in the past significant physical disabilities were successfully hidden from the general public. Polio victim Franklin Roosevelt was in office for nearly thirteen years and the public never saw him in a wheelchair or on his crutches!

President Kennedy on the "Cherry Picker" Time Inc. *(Reprinted with permission from Lynn Pelham/Getty Images)*

I was Appointments Secretary to Eisenhower the day the public was informed that he was in bed with a slight cold. I knew better. I had been standing before him at his desk in the Oval Office when he experienced what was later described as "an occlusion of a small branch of the middle cerebral artery." In layman's terms, Ike had had a stroke.

In addition to Addison's Disease, President Kennedy suffered from back problems so severe that his aides often placed a hospital bed in the White House movie theater so that he could enjoy watching films lying down. During Jack Kennedy's time as president, according to Dr. Jeffrey Kelman, the president was on ten medications a day, including codeine, Demerol™, methadone and daily injections of cortisone.

When out of camera view, President Kennedy frequently used crutches and walked downstairs sideways. Going up stairs was a bigger problem, and often when he had to board Air Force One he was lifted to the entrance by a cherry picker.

Incidentally, none of the above is meant to minimize the suffering of a man who bravely endured great pain most of his adult life. Rather, as with the other examples, it demonstrates how much of a president's life and private time is completely unknown to the voters.

President Eisenhower loved golf. More than once when I served as Ike's Appointments Secretary, Sherman Adams, the President's Chief of Staff, came into the office to speak with him only to find him absent, whereupon he would exclaim, "Good God, is he playing golf, again!" President Obama played 29 rounds of golf in his first year in office. So much for being tied to the desk.

Since Eisenhower loved golf, his schedule was filled with as many golf games as possible. Routinely, Ike came into the Oval Office whenever he had finished his breakfast and read the morning papers. He worked until about 11:45 a.m. and then went over to the mansion (the private quarters of the White House) for lunch. After lunch he returned to the office and continued meetings, or read his mail, until around 4 p.m. He then took off for a golf game or returned to the mansion for an evening with Mrs. Eisenhower or a game of bridge with pals from his days as Supreme Allied Commander.

After he left office, amateur artist Eisenhower admitted he had more time to paint when he was president, "because presidents are so fully supported and organized."As with everyone who works for a president, my job was to accommodate presidential demands and wishes. The important part of my job was to schedule necessary meetings with the President. The largest part of my time was spent on the telephone or in written correspondence, usually declining requests for presidential appointments from government officials, foreign diplomats, and private citizens whose requests could be handled by someone else.

It is easy to reminisce about a quieter and simpler time and categorize the Eisenhower Presidency as less stressful than today. However, this too is somewhat of a myth. Historians and us oldsters remember that during that time we had many significant challenges and that bomb shelters were being built across the land. The threat of a Russian military attack on the United States was so significant that the president and top White house officials had duplicate highly secret offices they could go to. They had been constructed in the bowels of a West Virginia mountainside. Without forewarning, the president, and those of us in select positions, would board helicopters on the South Lawn and carry out an evacuation drill. The wars were also not always "cold." During his two terms, President Eisenhower ordered U.S. troops to invade Lebanon. Ike also had many domestic challenges. He ordered the troops to Little Rock, Arkansas to enforce desegregation. He faced the competition with Russia in a new Space Age when the Soviets put Sputnik in orbit. Ike also created the national highway system and balanced the federal budget. These were not dulcet times.

Even so, when the editors of *U.S. News and World Report* asked us if they could do a photo essay entitled, "A Day in the Life of the President," it was a real effort to fatten up the presidential schedule to make it appear as if his workdays were indeed those of the so-called "busiest man in the world." And even though those were not simpler days, Eisenhower was supported by only a couple dozen top staff, compared with the 43 czars and 469 White House professional assistants on call to President Obama today.

Unlike his nine-to-five fellow citizens, a United States President does not have fixed office hours nor even set workdays. This is not to suggest presidents do not have enough work to keep them busy, but if they knew the realities, most professionals would trade schedules with the president in a heartbeat.

Look at George W. Bush's eight years in office. Of those 2,920 days as president, according to one record, he spent 487 days at Camp David and another 490 at his ranch in Crawford, Texas—almost a third of his time in office.

In fairness, and this book is not intentionally unfair to, or critical of, any of our presidents, George Bush liked to entertain foreign guests at his Texas ranch or at Camp David. Still, his out-of-office time would have been the envy of most of his fellow taxpayers. And his example underscores our point that, while the presidency of the United States is arguably the most significant leadership role in the world, its physical demands are less than the jobs held by most of a president's countrymen.

During President Obama's initial 365 days in office he made 160 flights on Air Force One, attended 28 political fundraisers, and seven campaign rallies outside of Washington. There were also 26 admitted vacation days, plus an additional 27 days at Camp David, while squeezing in 29 rounds of golf. How is all this possible? It would be an understatement to say that 21st Century presidents have lots of time away from the desk and plenty of help.

Until FDR's presidency, the regal old Executive Building next to the White House held all the offices of the government's executive branches. The staff of today's president completely fills the old Executive Building—now renamed the Eisenhower Executive Office Building—while also filling three large office buildings across Pennsylvania Avenue.

To help with the burdens of the presidency, today's commander-in-chief has a chief of staff, a press secretary, and other assistants who make rare appearances in the news. Since only these few are seen in the news, the public is generally unaware of the small army of unseen personal assistants who actually do a good measure of that job for him and might more accurately be called assistant or substitute presidents.

President Lincoln answered his own mail, but back then there were seldom more than 20 letters a day. Today, the White House has to process tens of thousands of letters and e-mails a day. In

2009, the budget just for screening the White House mail was over $25,000,000! With the White House estimate of over a million pieces of mail handled annually, basic math tells us that taxpayers are spending $25 to deal with each piece. And almost none of this mail or e-mail directly reaches the man to whom all are addressed.

The president is the only American who has his own personal zip code. Mail from family and close friends bears this code so that those letters will go directly to the chief executive. In most cases, as happened with President Reagan, the private zip code has to be changed from time to time as relatives and close friends yield to the pressure of their friends and share the number.

Unless a letter addressed to the president carries his secret zip code, the odds are overwhelming that he never will know of its contents. The rare exceptions are when the presidential speechwriters personalize the chief executive's remarks in a nationally-broadcast speech to warm them up with a folksy anecdote; for instance: "I received a letter the other day from little Timmy O'Brien in Akron, Ohio. Timmy wrote me that his mother…" That technique gives the impression that the president reads every letter addressed to him. Sure, and so does Santa Claus!

Other than letters used by a president to make these kinds of humanizing points in his speeches, a president sees only those that the person reading the letters believes will lift his day or give him a laugh. I once passed Eisenhower a letter from a young girl inviting him to her birthday party. "I am only asking a few guests," she wrote, "You, the Queen of England, and Lassie."

My first appointment in the Eisenhower White House was Director of Presidential Patronage where I was responsible for screening and recommending men and women for potential presidential appointments to lofty government positions. Recommendations came from United States Senators and Congressmen, from governors and private citizens. No matter how he or she had been recommended, unless a candidate passed my scrutiny, the president might never have become aware of the candidate's desire or availability.

It was a heady assignment for a thirty-year-old and it gave me a great deal of power in determining the membership of the Federal

Trade Commission, the next head of Veterans Affairs, or the ambassador to a foreign country, to name just a few positions. Of course, the president ultimately made his selection. But he made it from my approved list. If candidates did not get *by* me, they did not get *to* him. This situation was actually not some unique power given to me. It was the way things were done in Ike's administration, the way they had been done in previous administrations, and, frankly, the way they continue to be done today!

Another presidentially granted power I was given, as were all others on the senior White House staff, was crafting answers to letters in the bulging presidential mail bag. In Ike's time, as is true today, communications addressed to the president on a certain topic were diverted to a designated staff member for response in the president's name.

If, for example, someone wrote to President Eisenhower about an immigration matter (one of the subjects assigned to me) I would respond in the President's name. If you have ever written to the White House, this will look familiar to you, since my response was much the same as it would be, today: "Thank you for your communication to the President about _____. The President has asked me to inform you that _____." The President, of course, never saw the incoming communication, which was signed by me.

I composed and signed so many of these responses on Eisenhower's behalf that it seemed only fair when one day I had to respond to a frustrated repeat writer who very understandably asked in his letter: "Dear Mr. President, who the hell is Robert Gray?"

In addition to answering the bulk of a president's mail, staff members, especially senior members of a president's staff, also make many weighty decisions that then are attributed to the president. Senior staff members today have assumed such importance that they even have their own jets marked similarly to Air Force One.

Many staff members ride along on Air Force One when the president thinks he may need that person's expertise, or if he simply wants to give someone the special privilege of such prestigious recognition. Even when staff members are not needed onboard Air Force One itself, they frequently fly to the President's destination on one of four Boeing C-32A presidential staff planes. This is ostensibly in case the president needs their advice or input, but often it is really because this affords them a chance to network, raise funds, or campaign for various constituents and their re-election efforts, in the president's name.

There has been a steady increase in power on the part of the presidential sidekicks, not the last of which is their acceptance of gifts. Sherman Adams, Eisenhower's Chief of Staff, was forced to resign when it was disclosed that he had accepted the loan of a rug and the gift of a coat from a friend—even though that friend had been the best man at Adams' wedding. Since those years, the rules have relaxed significantly. For example, both Pepsi and the Coca Cola Company "comp" the presidential staff with all the sodas they can consume.

The Mars Company provides tons of its M&Ms, all bearing the presidential seal, for staff members to give to family, friends and White House visitors. Once that bar got lowered, makers of potato chips and energy bars—and just about everyone with a product to sell—have stepped forward to try to gain the prestige of advertising the use of their products in the White House.

Once you start relaxing the rules, it is hard to know where the gifting ends or how high it goes. President Lyndon Johnson did not like Coca Cola. He preferred Fresca. So for him the company not only supplied unlimited amounts of the soda but also installed a Fresca tap in the mansion.

There is always the worry that senior staff members will become so impressed with their duties that they conclude ordinary rules do not apply to them.

No wonder the duties of today's presidency can be dispatched with so little of the President's own personal, hands-on time. With nearly 500 "assistant presidents" running a large part of the government, the President has plenty of free time to attend political rallies, spend weeks at Martha's Vineyard, enjoy an eleven-day vacation in Hawaii, take his family and relatives on a jaunt to Rio, make a trip out West for fly-fishing in Yellowstone, spend four days in Chicago to play basketball, help out in several colleague's campaigns, visit a pub named in his honor in Ireland, fly all the way to Ohio to swear in local police officers, fly down to Florida so his family can watch the Space Shuttle launch, work in some golf, run up to Camp David, or just be totally out of the public eye, as President Obama was for 21 days last year!

"The spending binges by Obama during what is being called 'The Great Recession,' with as many as 20 percent of Americans actually out of work, wages stagnant, the price of gas increasing, the cost of food increasing, Obama makes no sacrifices and plunders the American treasury as he and Michelle live like kings and queens at the expense of the middle class and the poor American taxpayer."

—*The Knoxville Journal*, February 3, 2012

CHAPTER THREE

---◆·❖·◆---

When a Man's Home
Is His Castle, Literally

O ver the years, first families have added to, subtracted from, built on and even had parts of the White House demolished, without requesting permission to do so from either the American people or their representatives in Congress. They can do this, in what is only their temporary domicile, because we the people have, knowingly or not, given presidents the unfettered power to change 1600 Pennsylvania Avenue in any way they wish—and to acquire or sell off presidential "possessions."

President Teddy Roosevelt had a large family. He decided they needed more space, so he ordered the leveling of the greenhouses, which had dated back to the 1850s, to make room for the construction of the entire West Wing. It was planned to house some of his family, his small staff, the Secret Service and the presidential bowling alleys.

When you have extra space, you grow into it. FDR had six on his staff. By Eisenhower's Administration, the presidential staff had grown to 32 in the West Wing. President Reagan's staff had its offices in the West Wing and also in the Executive Office Building, which as I explained earlier, had in previous administrations housed all of the offices of the entire United States government. Growth of the White House compound has continued with every new administration. The staff that fills the West Wing, the Executive Office Building and a large number of new buildings across Pennsylvania Avenue now numbers 469 men and women—professionals only—not including many hundreds more on the secretarial and support staff.

The assistants to the president have their own impressive toys. The Presidential Staff Planes consist of four Boeing C-32A jets that would seat 189 when used in commercial service. Each has been refitted to provide spacious accommodations to a total of only 45 presidential staff members.

The growth in numbers of the presidential top staff has actually been small compared to the growth in value of many of the presidential perks, especially his transportation. Eisenhower's airplane, the Columbine, cost a little more than three million dollars. Today's Air Force One and its twin for backup purposes—which is known as "the Wannabe"—cost the taxpayers $640,000,000. That's nearly two thirds of a billion dollars. With 26 crew members and, again, FIVE full-time chefs, Air Force One and the "Wannabe" are the most luxurious airplanes in the world.

Marine One, the presidential helicopter, is actually not one helicopter, but a fleet of 35, all housed in a hanger that the Marine Corps calls "the Cage." On order are 28 more helicopters, to be known as Helicopter Squadron HmX-ONE, the Presidential Fleet, at a cost of $11 billion.

Another major perk is Camp David. Before 1942, Camp David was known as Hi-Catoctin, and was a camping area for the benefit of all federal employees and their families. Without any authorizing legislation or request for public approval, President Franklin Roosevelt summarily took over the property for the exclusive use of ONE federal employee—the president.

The White House swimming pool is another luxury with an interesting history. The dimes of American school kids contributed to the costs of construction of the original pool through annual drives by the March of Dimes, which is now focused on birth defects but originally raised money for polio research and related projects. President Roosevelt desperately needed its waters to exercise his polio-stricken limbs. The pool was built indoors in the wide building FDR erected to connect the new West Wing to the White House.

In later years, Eisenhower's White House guest, Winston Churchill, swam in it, and Jack Kennedy famously held skinny-dipping parties there. Lyndon Johnson also swam nude in the pool, and when staff members refused to swim in the buff, he referred to them as "the Harvards," which to Lyndon Johnson was the ultimate pejorative. When Richard Nixon served as president, he became obsessed with the thought that the press was out to destroy his presidency. In an attempt to ingratiate himself with the press corps, he decided to have the indoor swimming pool floored over and turned the entire area into a fancy lounge for members of the White House media.

Any subsequent president could have reversed President Nixon's decision, but that never happened. At one point, Gerald Ford did consider returning the pool to its original use, and was assured workmen could easily remove the floor and the tiled pool would be ready for filling. But Ford was also advised that if he did this, he would incur the enmity of the fourth estate. Neither he nor any subsequent president wanted to suffer that consequence. Instead, Ford ordered the White House to build a second pool—an outdoor, fully heated one, just outside the Oval Office, taking up what had been a large portion of the White House's famed Rose Garden.

We have given presidents total freedom to make any necessary changes in terms of décor, customs, structure and tradition. President Truman, in fact, undertook the most gigantic White House overhaul ever ordered by any president. In 1942, after he was advised that several parts of the White House needed shoring up, he ordered the entire interior gutted. It would have been an easier and far less expensive construction job to tear the whole building down and begin again. Instead, the outside walls were allowed to remain to shield the awesome extent of the destruction from the prying eyes of the public—even though they were footing the bill.

When Harry and Bess Truman occupied the White House, they spent most of their evenings in what is called the Yellow Oval Room. As the White House interior was being rebuilt, President Truman ordered that a balcony be constructed off his and Bess's favorite room. When architects and purists said the balcony would spoil the symmetry and appearance of the White House, Truman responded: "To

National Park Service photo of the gutted interior of a large por tion of the White House
(Photo with permission from Abbie Rowe, Courtesy of Harry S. Truman Library)

tell the truth, I don't give a damn." The deed was done, with no public vote. This balcony will always be known as the Truman Balcony.

The Iconic Presidential Yacht is Sold

Before President Hoover made the Sequoia the presidential yacht, it had been used by the Department of Commerce as a decoy to catch Prohibition lawbreakers. Herbert Hoover used it for his favorite sport, fishing. Over a span of forty-four years, the yacht became almost as much a part of presidential history as the White House.

U.S.S. Sequoia. As the yacht passed Mt. Vernon, the flag was dipped to symbolically salute George Washington. *(Printed with permission © Ann Stevens, All Rights Reserved)*

During World War II, Roosevelt secretly met on the Sequoia with Eisenhower, who was then the Supreme Allied Commander, to discuss D-Day invasion plans. Later Harry Truman had an upright piano put aboard and entertained political friends with his piano playing during poker games. It was aboard the Sequoia that Richard Nixon broke the news to his family that he had decided to resign. Lyndon Johnson enjoyed sitting on the upper deck to watch movies projected onto the Sequoia's white smokestack. And John F. Kennedy celebrated his last birthday aboard her.

In addition to all the family time presidents and first families spent aboard her, the Sequoia was invaluable as a tool for presidential negotiating. Aboard the Sequoia, official handshakes with foreign heads of state changed history. For use with recalcitrant members of Congress, the yacht had no equal. A president would board those Congressmen or Senators who had not committed to a certain piece of legislation and ply them with camaraderie and a few libations. Then the Sequoia's captain would set a course down the Potomac to George Washington's Mt. Vernon, where the yacht would drop anchor for a ceremonial salute, and the ship's trumpeter would play taps. By the time the Sequoia was back at its pier, the president's arm was around the shoulders of his former legislative adversaries, and deals had been struck.

So FDR took over what is now Camp David for exclusive presidential use, and President Truman gutted the White House and ordered construction of a balcony and a movie theater. President Nixon removed FDR's swimming pool, and President Ford ordered a new pool built. President George Bush Sr. had a jogging track installed, which President Bill Clinton later ordered torn up. Former U.S. Naval officer, President Jimmy Carter, summarily sold the presidential yacht without the approval of anyone—a perfect example of the totality of power our presidents have to add to or subtract from what is actually the people's property.

The White House Royal Grounds

The White House lawn itself, in addition to being meticulously manicured, provides fertile ground for getting across the first family's political and social messages. During World War II, Eleanor Roosevelt had a "victory garden "planted on the White House grounds to set an example for citizens to grow their own produce in food-short America. In the decades since, the land has "lain fallow," as they say in farm country when land is left unplanted to give it a chance to rejuvenate.

First Lady Michelle Obama had a five-acre piece of the White

House grounds turned over for a vegetable garden. She has reported that 740 pounds of food has been grown on this plot of land "at a cost of about $180." This project has great spirit and is a great model for America. And certainly the price seems like a bargain.

First Lady Michelle Obama and local elementary school students in White House vegetable garden, Oct. 2009.   *(Photo with permission Tim Sloan, AFP / Getty Images)*

But it should be noted that initially a crew from the United States Park Service had to remove 20 inches of topsoil from those five acres and replace it with "more virgin" dirt. Then they provided the seeds, the roto-tiller, the fertilizers and the heavy manpower. Taxpayers provided all that, and taxpayers will pay for the 24-hour security to keep this garden, unlike the one in your backyard, safe from rabbits, deer, or a neighbor's poaching. Of course the taxpayers also pay for the cultivating, weeding, fertilizing and harvesting of the garden, and pay the salary of the newly created position of White House "Farm Site Coordinator," as well as one of the four assistant White House chefs, whose civil service title designates him "White House Garden Overseer." Suddenly that crop becomes a little pricier than the symbol of prudent thriftiness it seemed to be.

To maintain the White House grounds, the Park Service employs a chief horticulturist plus three foremen, eight gardeners, and one maintenance operator. Additionally, more Park Service personnel are called in to work on trees, roads, maintenance, outdoor plumbing and electrical services. The Park Service also unclogs drains and commodes when necessary, maintains an adequate stock of supplies sufficient to replace items such as toilet paper, hand towels and soap, sweeps the White House Visitor Center, shovels snow and ice from walkways and spreads sand, salt or other chemicals to prevent people from slipping, and assists with trash removal. Last year the price tag for these chores was $6,241,000. The Park Service's operations at the White House provide an example of how to take a simple task like mowing grass and turn it into an expensive and excessive mini-bureaucracy.

Incidentally, did you ever wonder why your grass turns brown in the winter, while the verdant grass of the lawn at 1600 Pennsylvania Avenue always keeps its brilliant color? There's an easy answer: after the first frost, the taxpayers fund the National Park Service personnel's mandate to spray paint the entire lawn to keep the White House bluegrass green.

The White House as the President's Own Country Club

While youths at many inner-city schools must get their exercise on public courts strewn with broken glass, and even well-off Americans have, at best, a basketball hoop in their driveways, the President of the United States has a basketball court on the grounds of the mansion he calls home. First families and their guests can enjoy the many facilities of country-club caliber provided for them. These facilities also are useful for fundraising.

In fact, generous campaign supporters and potential contributors are frequent guests at the White House "country club." "I shot a few baskets today with the President at the White House," can be a great, albeit expensive, item to drop casually in conversation at a business meeting or social gathering.

Indeed, no expense has been spared to ensure that presidents and their guests can relax and play in style.

A Truly Regal Cinema

Another significant perk was added to the "castle" when President Truman ordered the conversion of a long East Wing coatroom into a movie theater. Now First Families could watch films around the clock. President Bill Clinton once said that the best of presidential perks was not Air Force One or Camp David but the White House movie theater, where presidential families and their guests can sit on luxurious lounge chairs in a beautiful chamber with the purest of acoustics to watch the movie they have summoned up—regardless of time of day or night.

Margaret Truman's favorite film was *The Scarlett Pimpernel*. She ordered it so many times that the movie operator claimed he had memorized all the lines of every actor in the movie. Eisenhower loved Westerns and screened more than 200 films in his eight years in office. His favorite was Gary Cooper's *High Noon*, a film also watched more often than any other by succeeding presidents.

When the theater was first used, its forty well-upholstered seats and the four massive armchairs in the front row for first family members were covered in stark white fabric. They later were covered in green until Nancy Reagan ordered the room converted to red, which was her favorite color.

During his presidency, Jack Kennedy's back problems made it difficult for him to watch films. Usually his aides replaced the overstuffed chair reserved for commanders in chief with JFK's famous rocking chair. On a few occasions, when his back pains were really severe, an orthopedic bed was brought in so that President Kennedy could watch a film propped up on pillows.

Lyndon Johnson was not much into films, although many times he particularly enjoyed watching and re-watching the 10-minute tribute to him that had been made on White House orders to introduce his new presidency to a skeptical public after the Kennedy assassination.

Richard Nixon always watched a movie when his best friend, Bebe Rebozo, was in town. The two of them saw 150 movies together. The only repeat for them was *Patton*.

Jimmy Carter saw a staggering 450 movies in the White House

theater, which averages to one every three nights he was in office. The first movie he watched was *All the President's Men* about the Watergate scandal that helped bring him into office. Interestingly, devout Baptist Carter was the first president to see an X-rated movie in the theater when he ordered *Midnight Cowboy.*

President Obama holds White House Super Bowl Party, Feb. 2, 2009.   *(Photo with permission from Pete Souza /White House via Getty Images)*

During their White House years, Ronald and Nancy Reagan mostly watched movies when they were spending a weekend at Rancho del Cielo, their ranch in California, or at Camp David. During President Reagan's birthdays in the White House, Nancy usually ordered one of his old films to be shown. On those occasions, when guests were present, Reagan sometimes made side comments about the art of air kissing or the bad breath of the actress with whom he had been paired in the film on the screen.

President Clinton had an eclectic taste in films, ordering everything from serious thought-provokers like *Schindler's List* to slapsticks like *Naked Gun*. Clinton also liked the White House's most-watched film, *High Noon*, and recommended to George W.

Bush that he see it as his first movie in the White House theater. In his first year in office, Bush II especially enjoyed the slapstick Austin Powers films. After 9/11, his tastes turned more to war films.

People in the movie industry have been among the strongest supporters of President Obama's candidacy. When the Obamas use the theater their guests often include the producers and stars of the films they show.

Michelle Obama acknowledges national anthem as the President waves to friends at Kennedy Center Honors *(Photo with permission from Jim Watson/Getty Images)*

Compared to the 450 times President Carter used the movie theater in his four years in the White House, the average American citizen, according to industry statistics, goes out to see a movie slightly less than five times a year. Taxpayers have to stand in line and may have had to save up or spend lunch money to take their families to a flick. Those same taxpayers provide first families with free admission to the country's plushest boutique theater. To insure that movies are available for the first family and invited guests to watch around the clock, literally 24 hours a day, projectionists sleep in the mansion so that one will always be on call.

Another Gift that Keeps on Giving

Speaking of the President's ties to (and support from) Hollywood and many of those in the arts, President and Mrs. Obama, in addition to private and exclusive use of the best movie theater in America, also enjoy another entertainment-related bonanza: perpetual full access—not just for themselves, but also for friends and supporters—to the best seats at Washington's premier entertainment showpiece, the Kennedy Center.

Referred to as the Presidential Loge, this section is located in the box tier just a few seats away from where the recipients of the Kennedy Center Honors are seated for that world-class event. This special Honors program is seen by the general public at least once a year on television. The president and first lady are always personally present to grace those awards with their presence, surrounded by the year's recipients for their efforts in performances on stage, in film and in the field of music.

Considering that they have their own entertainment center in the White House, presidents and their families tend not to use the loge seats often for their own personal entertainment. However, they do make good use of the campaign value of sitting in "the Presidential Box" for various performances and functions. While the box is reserved for presidential use at each and every performance, it is more often friends and large financial contributors to the seated president's campaign for re-election who are granted the highly visible privilege of attending shows—often treating their own friends to these seats—in this very special suite at the Center.

Front-row seating isn't the only great part of this experience. . Guests enter a moderately large anteroom where they find several chairs covered in striped silk, an end table with a lighted mirror, and several oil paintings by famous artists for them to appreciate. They also have the Presidential Seal on several items to remind them of their patron, and a refrigerator stocked with champagne bearing the same seal and labeled as "Presidential" bubbles. Needless to say, popping the cork on a bottle of fine champagne is all the more exciting given the fact that the attendees are being treated by the current president at a center named after one of the most celebrated of presidents. This is an excellent example of the many honors bestowed upon the acting commander-in-chief that he can in turn bestow upon various dignitaries, friends and, of course, donors to his campaign.

"Dozens of Obama's elite donors—many of them wealthy business figures—have been appointed to advisory panels and commissions that can play a role in setting government policy. Others have been invited to a range of exclusive White House briefings, holiday parties and splashy social events."

—iWatchNews by the Center for Public Integrity,
January 19, 2012

CHAPTER FOUR

———◆•◆•◆———

An Insider Tour of the Presidential Palace and Grounds

The White House was not a posh palace in our country's early history. In fact, Thomas Jefferson called living in the White House "a splendid misery." Andrew Jackson saw it as "dignified slavery." Even as recent a president as Harry S. Truman referred to it as "the big white jail." But as you have already seen in the earlier chapters, the White House and its attendant luxurious perks have grown expansively over the decades. Today, it accurately fits Gerald Ford's description as "the best public housing in America," or Ronald Reagan's perfect description, "an eight-star hotel."

Living free in the White House literally means living for free. Of course, the first family pays no rent. Unlike most every other tax-paying family, the first family doesn't pay for help, electricity, air conditioning, heating, insurance, taxes, repairs and the cost of furnishing, maintenance, upkeep or cleaning. Today, our presidents and their families have exclusive and free use of all but five rooms of a 132-room mega-mansion that encompasses 55,000 square feet on 18 acres of the most valuable, non-oil bearing land in America. If the property were for sale, according to our nation's top realtors, its value would be somewhere between a quarter and a third of a billion dollars. Also, unlike every other job in the United States in which housing happens to be included as part of the employment package, the Internal Revenue Service assigns no tax value to the president's free use of this finest of residences.

In this most elegant setting, presidents and their families are assisted 24 hours a day by personal doctors, dentists, pharmacists, chefs, valets (the President's valet is reportedly paid $100,000 a year), maids, dressers, flower arrangers, nannies, chauffeurs, projectionists, pet handlers and more guards than the combined security forces of the Louvre, Versailles and the Vatican!

While the public believes the White House consists of three stories, it is in fact many more. There is one floor hidden behind the parapets above what appears, from the street, to be the roof, and officials will admit that there are "more than two" subterranean levels which, for security reasons, are never shown or detailed to the public.

The White House really is not white. When painters arrive to give it a face-lift, they use 300 gallons of what, according to the color charts, is white-white-gray. Technically, the White House is off-white.

In the mansion's four above ground levels are 132 rooms, including 16 bedrooms and 35 bathrooms (none open to the touring public), along with 28 fireplaces, 8 staircases and 3 elevators.

A common misconception is that the first family is squeezed into a small portion of the west end on the fifth floor. The residential area is actually enormous. First families can choose to bring their own furniture from home to make them feel more comfortable. They can also elect to use furniture from historical gems in storage in the White House attic. Depending on the first family's wishes, there are usually two or more sofas, several overstuffed chairs, an assortment of armchairs, two or more tables, lamps, television sets, etc. These pieces are of the highest value, set on priceless rugs, and surrounded by silk draperies and historic works of art.

Much of the White House furniture has come from wealthy donors. Grace Coolidge urged her husband, Calvin, to back a congressional resolution to permit the White House to receive rare old pieces as gifts to the mansion. Spurred by generosity, the opportunity for "bragging rights," and perhaps some handsome tax credits, the well-to-do have provided a flood of historical and priceless items. In all, there are more than 14,000 pieces of furniture, china, silver and artwork in the White House that are considered of inestimable or historic value.

South of the private living area are the first lady's massive bedroom, the first lady's office, the first lady's dressing room with vast closet spaces, the president's own palatial bedroom and the great Yellow Oval Room, which some presidents have called a study, but which most first families use as a second living room.

North of the family living room are three more very large first family bedrooms with adjacent sitting rooms, the president's 20 x 30-foot dining room, and an elevator to transport the first family downstairs to an exclusive, even larger private dining room on the floor below.

These spaces take up two-thirds of the floor, measuring approximately 6,000 square feet. Compare that to your own home size. The national average is less than 1800 square feet and in many urban areas some people make do with 300 square feet facing a brick wall—a fraction of the size of even the smallest presidential dining room. But presidential living space does not stop there.

During the Reagan Administration, the central hall was transformed into a spacious double drawing room. Its excellent furnishings are set on fine carpet; the walls hold magnificent oil paintings or watercolors, and valuable urns of deep green foliage and beautifully arranged flowers are everywhere. The wide corridor is also warmly lighted with crystal chandeliers and handsome table lamps.

There is ample room, just in this attractive corridor, for a cocktail reception of 300 close friends or financial supporters. It is in this corridor, alongside the elevator entrance, that the usher generally leaves the many gifts that flow in each and every day. Those of high value are intended to go to the State Department for storage in the vaults, but some of them eventually end up in presidential libraries. Jacqueline Kennedy reportedly coveted the jewels in a ceremonial dagger that had been presented to her husband by a Saudi King and tried to pry them out.

Gifts of lesser value may be kept by the first family. They range from articles of clothing, some of them haute couture, for example, Hermes ties and imported leather shoes, to expensive sets of golf clubs, electronic products and personal inventions. The gifts cover an interesting range from humorous to folksy to just plain worthless.

They may include jars of jelly, homemade Afghans, or crocheted coasters embroidered with the American flag. When the Bush dog, Millie, had pups, Barbara Bush received hundreds of dog bowls, many of them monogrammed.

The first family also has use of the great Yellow Oval Room and the Treaty Room. However, the first family is not limited to even these giant spaces. On the eastern third of the fifth floor are the Lincoln Suite, the Monroe Suite (a bedroom and large sitting room) and the Rose Suite, known as the Queens' Rooms. For one hundred and fifty years, American presidents have used these suites to house foreign guests. The pink Queens' Suite received its designation after Britain's Queen Elizabeth II and the Queen mother, the Netherlands' Queen Wilhelmina, and Greece's Queen Frederica stayed in it during their state visits. The public supposes this part of a first family's space is reserved for visiting heads of state, but this is not how it actually works.

Obviously, foreign heads of state do not just drop by. If a foreign leader wishes to pay a visit, his foreign office contacts the American ambassador in his country expressing a willingness to visit, if invited. Depending on a president's mood or a particular rough spot in U.S. relations with a foreign country, the foreign leader is invited to make a State Visit on a specified date.

Today, unless a visiting foreign leader happens to be a very close personal friend of the president, he/she and retinue are accommodated not in the White House but rather in Blair House. These VIP guest quarters consist of four connected townhouses for a combined total of 70,000 square feet. With more square feet than the White House, Blair House has 119 rooms, four dining rooms, a gym, a flower shop and a hair salon. Only a few hundred feet northwest from the White House, Blair House is so often used to put up visiting heads of state that it has become known as the President's Guest House on Pennsylvania Avenue. When occupied by a foreign head of state, that nation's flag flies atop Blair House and the property technically, if temporarily, becomes the territory of that nation.

Since the other rooms on the fifth floor of the White House are no longer used for foreign dignitaries, the first family can, and does, use them personally. If the first lady wants, she can make the Rose Room her own and can let a relative, friend or contributor sleep in one of the Queens' Rooms. A president's children can also play house in the Lincoln Bedroom, or play jacks on the carpet or bounce on the 9 x 6-foot Lincoln Suite bed. Very little is sacred, and what the public thinks of as possibly "cordoned off " for state visits is very much at the first family's disposal. You might be surprised at how informal first families have been in making themselves at home. Pat Nixon smoked cigarettes in the private quarters, but when her husband wanted to enjoy a cigar, she sent him to the easternmost end of the floor to smoke his stogies in the Lincoln Sitting Room.

President Clinton invited many big givers to enjoy overnight stays in the Lincoln Bedroom. Nancy Reagan bunked Frank and Barbara Sinatra in the Queens' Suite. One of President Ford's sons was said to have boasted of entertaining a girlfriend on the big four-poster bed in the Queens' Suite.

As you can see, far from being restricted to one end of the White House, the entire and enormous fifth floor is for the exclusive use of the first family, either personally or to accommodate first family relatives, guests, campaign contributors or friends.

In addition to all that space on the fifth floor, plus the movie theater and presidential library on the third floor, plus the larger first family private dining room on the fourth floor, the first family also enjoys exclusive use of the atrium and the entire sixth floor. On that sixth floor are 20 more bedrooms, a large corridor, nine bathrooms, an exercise room and a game room with billiard and ping-pong tables. Relatives and the first family's young children and sleepover guests, unless they are given the Queen's Rooms or the Lincoln Suite, usually have their rooms on the sixth floor.

There are also some "gems" on the top floor: the Red Sitting Room and an octagonal Solarium with three walls of glass that is so large and light-filled that Mrs. Coolidge called the Solarium the "Sky Parlor."

Curious presidential guests quartered in the Queens' Rooms have discovered the hidden door that opens onto a staircase accessing the Solarium. A ramp from the Solarium leads to the top floor of the White House where presidents get to hone their bar-beque skills away from prying eyes and where young members of first families and their friends can sunbathe in private.

In addition to its bountiful spaces on the top two floors, the first family has exclusive use of the large family dining room on the fourth floor and likewise, on the third floor, the 50-loge-seat movie theater, the Map Room, the China Room, the Vermeil Room and the White House Library. None of these rooms are open to the public.

First families are quick to point out that, of all the domiciles housing the world's heads of state, "their" White House is the only such residence open to the public. They say that it is often referred to as the "Peoples' House," but as you can see, that's strictly not so.

Security concerns dictate that when the public is allowed on sightseeing tours (excluding the private areas, residential suites and other extensively restricted areas) visits are always regimented in the extreme. Limited members of the public can walk past (but not into) the president's movie theater, past (but not into) the historic China Room, past (but not into) the Vermeil Room, past (but not into) the White House Library, past (but not into) the Diplomatic Reception Room, and past (but not into) the large family dining area north of the State Dining Room.

Like hidden parts of a castle or manor house, the public does not get to see the unmarked door in a long corridor that stretches between two busts of World War II era allied leaders, Sir Winston Churchill and Dwight D. Eisenhower. This same door allows the president to access the nearby Treasury Building through a labyrinth of storage rooms and hallways. The passage also allows private traffic to flow the other way and has become known as "the Marilyn door" since the administration of President Kennedy.

Tourists are limited to the eastern corridor until they are directed up the stairway to the fourth level, where they pass through the East Ball Room, the Green Room, the Red Room, the Blue Room and the State Dining Room. After their requests to take pictures have been denied, they are shuffled out through the north portico, having seen only a small token of this seat of power and privilege.

In essence, out of 132 rooms, the public sees only two corridors, the entrance hall and five pristine showcase rooms. The rooms the public sees are beautiful and historic, but they fail to convey just how extensive and lavish the president's palace is! Additionally, this miniscule part of the White House is only open for some 20 hours each week, and to only a small sampling of the public.

For the remainder of the time, the whole estate is the first family's to enjoy in total privacy. They are free to entertain their friends in any part of it. They enjoy the lavish decorations, priceless paintings and exquisite objects d'art; they can lounge on the hidden balconies and hallways or bask in the sunlight in the Solarium. They can even let their kids ride their bikes in its corridors, play "Chopsticks" on the Steinway grand piano in the East Ballroom, or curl up in a museum-quality lounge in the Red Room, if that is where they want to play their video games or use their laptop computers.

But personal use isn't the only way that the first family benefits from the mansion facilities at their disposal. Susan Ford invited her classmates to have their junior prom in the East Room. Chelsea Clinton had her friends join her for pizza in the West Dining Room.

Of course, the first lady also can invite over anyone she would like to have for tea in her choice of any room. If the friend would like, he or she can sit under Gilbert Stuart's portrait of George Washington, or an original Whistler or dine beside Hassan's flag-bedecked masterpiece, *Avenue in the Rain*. Any arrangement the first lady wants can be accommodated; just as the Surveyor of the Royal Collections is at Queen Elizabeth's beck and call, the National Portrait Gallery has never refused a first lady's request to promptly provide any of its masterpieces "on loan."

But relaxing and entertaining are not the only concessions the White House makes to the personal needs of the first family. Off the massive corridor on the ground floor is the office of the presidential physician and his assistants (five military physicians, five nurses, five assistants, three medics and three administrators!). Along with a fully-stocked pharmacy, these medical professionals are available 24 hours a day, not just to the first family but to anyone staying in the White House or just visiting during the day. There is no waiting for appointments or dragging themselves to a doctor's office or a drugstore, no need to present an insurance card or Medicare form.

For anything from a Tylenol to open-heart surgery, taxpayers always foot the bill.

However, first families do not get everything for free: they do pay the costs of their own groceries and toiletries. This lone remnant from days when presidents were required to pay their own way was instituted by Congress during George Washington's administration. It has been maintained by Congress ever since—perhaps it makes members of Congress feel they have not surrendered every shred of control.

There are also several belowground levels of the White House. Although comfortable, they are not luxurious, but they represent the extreme safeguards the president and first family enjoy every second that they are at home. For security reasons, little is written about these rooms and they are never shown to the public. Underneath a bombproof edifice, however, bunker conditions hardly prevail. Rather, even if nuclear attack were leveling the rest of the Capitol for miles around, the president and his family and cabinet would be protected—not just from the blast, but from having to do without the services and surroundings they're so used to. Below ground at the White House are extensive living accommodations and work spaces, which may not compare with the mansion above but are nonetheless much nicer and far roomier than the homes of most Americans. Utilities that are independent of the main power grid, stocks of food and other necessities, and first-rate communications technology are all there for the first family's protection and comfort—not just for the preservation of presidential authority during an emergency.

One national treasure that will be preserved in such an emergency is the White House wine cellar, maintained under climate-controlled conditions. Since the Ford Administration, only domestic wine has been purchased for this cellar, although the collection predates this patriotic commitment to our country's vintners. Perhaps most famously, and almost unbelievably, the White House cellars still include a surprising number of bottles purchased in France and put up in the White House by Thomas Jefferson when he was president. Thus Jefferson's contribution to our national heritage was not limited to the bargain price at which he sold his book collection to the Library of Congress; in all, Jefferson invested $10,000 of his own money in fine wines, considering it appropriate for even a president to entertain at his own expense. That's about a quarter of a million in today's dollars.

A lot of wine also equates to a lot of wine bottles to be dusted. From tip to toe, the White House would always pass a white glove test. Whether it's underground bunkers or sky parlors or private balconies, the Presidential Palace is kept spotless. Keeping all the personal and public spaces pristine—even while they are in constant use—is a big job. Not to worry: the taxpayers pay for servants to do all that work.

But dusting, polishing and vacuuming aren't the only tasks about which the first family never has to worry. Presidents over the years have accrued a berth of specialists that probably match, person for person, the appointed specialists in any of Europe's royal households: gardeners, painters, curators, hairstylists, and butlers. Even florists are on retainer for the president (with the exception of the Polk Administration, when flowers were banned in the belief they gave off unhealthy vapors and robbed the air of valuable elements). Taxpayers foot the bill (usually about a quarter of a million dollars each year) for fresh flowers to be arranged daily in several dozen vases throughout the White House.

There are servants assigned to personal tasks too. There are the president's valets and the first lady's maids, and backups of these servants who are fully trained and well rehearsed in the personal preferences of their master and mistress. It would not be right to say "their employers" for their employers are you and me—the taxpayers. Even the children's nannies have backups in case the mainstays are sick or absent. (If you think that sort of luxury is downright regal for the people in a democracy's White House, then you may bristle over Chapter 7, in which we describe the attentions lavished on the First Canine by a full-time dog handler.)

The personal catering is nothing short of regal. Often, presidents find they have come to take it so completely for granted that once they exit office, they are startled by the way their citizens live their lives. They even wonder how the average person manages to function! The author met with former President Eisenhower on the first morning after he left the White House at the end of his two terms. "This morning," Ike said proudly, flashing his famous grin, "I picked out my own tie!" Or, as Nancy Reagan wrote honestly in her memoir *My Turn*, "Every evening, while I took a bath, one of the maids would come by and remove my clothing for pressing or dry cleaning. The bed would always be turned down. Five minutes after Ronnie had come home and hung up his suit, it would disappear from the closet to be pressed or cleaned." No wonder Reagan called the White House an eight-star hotel.

While HRH Queen Elizabeth is never seen in public without her purse, it is said she never carries any cash or personal identification. Why should she? Similarly, our President is never asked to display a driver's license, purchase his own newspaper, hail a cab, pick up dry cleaning, tip a waiter, pay a utility bill, choose his own necktie or turn down his own sheets. It is easy to imagine the extent to which the first family falls out of touch with the minor interactions and chores that even well-to-do Americans face on a daily basis—to say nothing of the monetary expenses they are spared by this treatment.

Think of all your other nuisances and costs that we cover for our president and his family:

Moving-in expenses:	No charge to First Family
Heat, light, air conditioning:	No charge to First Family or their guests.
High speed Internet access:	No charge to First Family or their guests.
Laundry services:	No charge to First Family or their guests.
Cooks, waiters:	No charge to First Family or their guests.
Cleaning services:	No charge to First Family or their guests.
Local and international telephone:	No charge to First Family or their guests.
Periodicals and newspapers:	No charge to First Family or their guests.
All TV channels and cable:	No charge to First Family or their guests.

Total medical care:	No charge to First Family or their guests.
Prescriptions:	No charge to First Family or their guests.
Personalized stationery, pens:	No charge to First Family or their guests.
Transportation:	No charge to First Family or their guests.
Motion Pictures:	No charge to First Family or their guests.
Baby-sitting services:	No charge to First Family or their guests.
Pet caring services:	No charge to First Family or their guests.
WH athletic facilities:	No charge to First Family or their guests.
Massage therapist:	No charge to First Family or their guests.
Presidential Seal terry bathrobes:	No charge to First Family or their guests.
Real Estate taxes:	No charge to the First Family.
Property Insurance:	No charge to the First Family.
	(In fact, there is no insurance policy on the White House. If it burns down, the taxpayers will rebuild it!)
Moving out expenses:	No charge to the First Family

In sum, presidents live without having to pay for housing, transportation or even entertainment. They have full and exclusive use of the facilities of a fully-equipped "country club," without any dues and assessments! They make no payment for full medical services for themselves and their families. They are never bothered with utility bills or the costs of petty subscriptions and contracts, such as for newspapers or television. The presidential lifestyle is wholly sheltered from the myriad disbursements that pile up for most of us along with business taxes, office rent, secretarial help, the costs of computers, telephones and fax machines, or even office supplies. In fact, unless a president wants to buy a gift for his wife or a trinket for himself, he never even needs to carry cash or a credit card.

There have been a lot of changes and a lot of luxury added into the mix in the years since First Lady Abigail Adams did her own laundry and hung it in the East Room to dry—even while she closely advised and consulted with her husband in person and by correspondence throughout his time as president.

Harry Truman ran the renovated White House with a total staff of 285, while going toe-to-toe with the entire Soviet Empire. Even the Kennedy's much vaunted style was managed with the assistance of a mere 375 persons. By George W. Bush's time, the White House staff had escalated to over 1,100. But two years into the Obama Administration, the payroll had increased by another 10% to over 1,200!

It is nearly impossible to track the full expenses of employees assigned to the White House mansion. Instead, some White House expenses are buried in departmental budgets and various appropriations bills, with classified portions of their own. Still, even a cursory look into some budget disclosures is revealing. For example, even without the cost of real estate taxes or insurance costs, the General Government Appropriations Act of 2008 puts the annual operating expense of the White House mansion at $12,814,000—which, divided by 365 days, gives us a White House mansion operating expense of $35,100 a day! While that amount supposedly covers the maintenance and services in the mansion and its grounds, another $1,600,000 was set aside in the 2008 budget for White House repair and restoration.

According to Bradley H. Patterson's excellently researched book, *To Serve the President*, the total cost to the taxpayers of all White House elements for fiscal year 2008—and this figure includes such items as security and White House professionals—was over one and a half billion dollars. That's nearly four million dollars a day. In contrast, to keep Elizabeth II on the throne in royal style costs United Kingdom taxpayers a bit less than 60 million dollars annually, while revenues from the Crown's Estate return about 300 million dollars to the British Treasury.

"Is there anyone in the White House with nerve enough to tell Barack Obama that Martha's Vineyard is the last place on earth that [he] should find himself...Camp David comes equipped with 24-hour guard service, including fighter jets...For presidential enjoyment, Camp David's wooded mountain-top has a swimming pool, a sauna, tennis courts, a bowling alley, a trout stream and movie facilities...Plus there are guest cottages should the Obamas wish to have friends over. And, of course, highly trained chefs...Ah, but that seems to be not enough when stacked against Cape Cod."

—Colbert I. King in *The Washington Post*, August 12, 2011

CHAPTER FIVE

———◆◆◆◆◆———

Camp David: A Vacation Retreat for Family, Friends and Political Contributors

C amp David, the rustic 125-acre presidential retreat, is part of the Catoctin Mountain Park recreational area in Frederick County, Maryland, 60 miles north of Washington, D.C. It was founded by President Franklin D. Roosevelt as Shangri-La and later renamed Camp David after Dwight Eisenhower's grandson.

When President Roosevelt directed the purchase of Hi-Catoctin for $25,000, it was a park set aside for the use of federal employees and their families. Today, the 130-acre mountain retreat, now called Camp David, is reserved for the exclusive use of one federal employee and one federal employee only, the President of the United States, and those relatives, foreign dignitaries, friends or political contributors he favors with an invitation.

It took no Act of Congress to authorize conversion of the facility from a recreational retreat enjoyed by all federal employees into an encampment devoted solely to the exclusive use of the president and those with whom he offers to share it. It was not something championed by the public or by the press or by proclamation or referendum vote of the American taxpayers. As in all cases of presidential perks, it only took one vote to make it happen: that of the Chief Beneficiary himself.

On a few high-profile occasions, each president will use Camp David to entertain a foreign visitor, or to hammer out an important international accord, in a natural (and highly security-friendly) environment. More often than not, however, he will use it for personal recreation.

Unlike first family's private stays at Camp David, use of the facility when there is an international visitor present always receives big coverage in the news media. Therefore, most taxpayers think Camp David is regularly used for matters of national and international importance. In truth, Camp David has been used to host foreign visitors on only a few dozen occasions since 1942, the year FDR took over the Camp for the exclusive use of presidents. During the 21,000-plus days since then, only first families and their lucky foreign or domestic guests (or campaign contributors) have enjoyed the vast complex provided so freely by the largess of us taxpayers.

The athletic Kennedy family loved to play touch football on Camp David's lawns and on its acres of rolling hills and perfectly groomed fields. Rosalynn and Jimmy Carter liked to picnic beneath the mighty oaks on the mossy banks of one of the rolling streams, or ride bicycles through the nature trails. After a fresh snow, Gerald Ford liked to race a snowmobile around Camp David, surrounded by the beauty of landscaped forests and an assortment of carefully planted and cared-for trees. And, since the figure-eight swimming pool is heated to 72-degrees year-round, including in winter, President Ford would encourage his dogs to go in the pool for a dip.

Excellent horsemen, Nancy and Ronald Reagan liked to ride off the trails and explore new paths, even outside the security fences. George H.W. Bush liked to pitch horseshoes at Camp David. His family loved the place so much that daughter Doro chose to have her wedding at Camp David instead of at the White House. And son George W. Bush spent no fewer than 487 of his days as President at Camp David. That's more than one full year out of his eight years in office!

President Obama and the First Family boarded Marine One to make their first 30-minute flight up to Camp David only *three* days after the President was inaugurated, then spent 27 more days there—all within his first year in office! And, since at least three helicopters are involved in a trip to Camp David, at the Marine Corps' operating cost estimate of $8,450 an hour, each roundtrip a president makes to the Camp costs the taxpayers $25,350. And that is only for the fuel!

It may surprise a reader to learn that at all times there are one hundred and fifty military personnel at Camp David. It may be an even greater surprise to learn that when the president is in residence, the number of personnel tasked with supporting and serving him and his guests or his family can swell to four hundred, not counting the Secret Service men and women!

These are not added Secret Service men and women responsible for guarding the president and his guests; these are *extra* military personnel, largely Seabee members of the Navy, who are there to maintain the Camp—literally, to tend to everything from its plumbing, electrical, air conditioning and heating needs, or to act as waiters and cooks, and otherwise serve the first family and any guests they bring along. The payroll just for the military staff at Camp David to serve the First Family was over $8,000,000 in 2009! These expenses, like most expenses for the benefit of presidents, are conveniently cloaked in the "expenses" of other departments or bureaus or agencies. In this case, it is among the Seabee subsection of the appropriation for the United States Navy's part of the Defense Department's budget. If that is not deliberate obfuscation, it certainly is a convenient way to frustrate a writer trying to put an accurate figure on the cost of our presidency.

So what is this costing us? In his book, *The $1.8 Billion Dollar Man*, John F. Groom estimated the combined transportation and personnel costs of a president's visit to Camp David to be $295,000 per night.

If a president had to pay for Camp David visits from his own pocket, wouldn't you agree the odds are great that he more often than not would find a way to make do with the 137 rooms of the White House and its country club facilities?

"On June 28, 2011, Judicial Watch filed a FOIA request seeking the mission taskings, transportation records, and passenger manifests for Michelle Obama's Africa trip...Judicial Watch calculated the total cost to American taxpayers was $424,142 for use of the aircraft...The expense records also show $928.44 was spent for "bulk food" purchases on flight. Overall, during the trip, 192 meals were served for the 21 passengers on board...'This junket wasted tax dollars and the resources of our overextended military. No wonder we had to sue to pry loose this information,' said Judicial Watch President Tom Fitton."

—*US News & World Report*, October 4, 2011

CHAPTER SIX

———◆·•◆·•◆———

The First Lady's Queenly Prerogatives

B ecause the first lady officially serves the nation in her capacity as hostess of the White House and receives no compensation for that service, who can deny her some special perks of her own, like designer dresses and make-up artists on call for every occasion? Most people would agree that she deserves the accoutrements she needs to make a favorable impression in public and on state occasions. Nonetheless, taxpayers should be aware of the wildly disproportionate increase in the First Lady's perks and distaff budget since 1789, when Martha Washington first represented the country in this capacity.

All the first ladies who held that position up until the time of Bess Truman had no special help, unless their husbands paid for it out of his own incomes. Mamie Eisenhower's secretary was paid out of President Eisenhower's salary.

First Lady Michelle Obama has a staff of some twenty individuals to help her with the pressures of her role as hostess of the White House and mother of two.

It is a matter of public record that Mrs. Obama's chief of staff is paid $172,200. Four others on her staff are paid between $114,000 to $140,000. All told, Mr. Obama's staff budget last year was nearly a million and a half dollars! It may be hard for out-of-work Americans to believe these figures, but if the king is spending money like there's no tomorrow, why should his queen feel inhibited?

In addition to permanent staff members, Michelle Obama, in her capacity as first lady, also has on-call services of hair stylist Johnny Write, and make-up artist Ingrid Grimes-Miles. Both are paid on a part-time basis and get to travel with the First Lady on Air Force One.

As I reported earlier, in addition to the twin Air Force Ones, there is a group of large jets known as "the Presidential Fleet." During Easter week, 2011, Michelle Obama and Jill Biden, wife of the Vice President, traveled together to New York for a fun-filled fling and a television appearance on the popular daytime television program *The View*. Returning to Andrews Air Force Base outside Washington, they were traveling in a Boeing 737 from the Presidential Fleet when its landing was aborted because it was too close to the flight path of a C-19 cargo plane.

This mishap led the Federal Aeronautics Administration to decree that, in the future, all flights taken by the First Lady or the "Second Lady" (as the wife of the vice president is sometimes called) would be handled by an air traffic supervisor, not just a mere flight-path controller, the person who handles flights for Joe Publics like you and me. Most people who fly on a regular basis have been onboard a plane whose landing was aborted or delayed due to the usual safety precautions that are ably handled by our nation's well supervised flight traffic controllers. But when a first lady's televised hoopla-fest results in what is, in essence, a typical occurrence, whole departments of our federal government change their protocol to make sure she will not be inconvenienced again.

First Lady Michelle Obama drew flack from the media and irate citizens when it was disclosed that, not counting Saturdays and Sundays, she spent 42 days on vacation—within the span of one year. And not only did she enjoy more vacation time than the average American, she also took "40 of her closest friends" (source: her own White House spokesman) on a vacation trip to Marbella, Spain, where Michelle Obama and her retinue occupied more than sixty of the best rooms in the super-elegant Villa Padierna Hotel. For this trip, Mrs. Obama used the C-3A (a Boeing 757 jumbo jet), an airplane that serves as Air Force Two, the lookalike or "Wannabe" to Air Force One. Like most of the expenses connected with the First Family, it is impossible to get an accurate accounting, but using the best estimates available to him, a top-ranking Defense Department representative estimated that the cost to taxpayers for this one excursion was over a million dollars—and this was just for operation of the aircraft.

The extravagance of this trip prompted the *New York Daily News* to headline its story, "Material Girl Michelle Obama is a modern-day Marie Antoinette," a reference to the French royal who lived in luxury

First Lady Michelle Obama, daughters Sasha and Malia, mother Marian Robinson, niece Leslie Robinson and nephew Avery Robinson on safari in the Madikwe Game Preserve, South Africa. June 25, 2011. *(Photo with permission from AP Photo/Charles Dharapak, Pool)*

while the people of France suffered in fiduciary doldrums. The First Lady also took vacations to Panama City and other locations in Latin America, to Martha's Vineyard, to Hawaii, to South Africa, and to the elite ski-resort towns of Vail, Colorado and Corvallis, Oregon.

There was criticism when Mrs. Obama took several of her relatives and friends on a trip to South Africa and Botswana—a trip estimated to cost taxpayers between $700,000 and $800,000, not including the expenses incurred by Mrs. Obama's staff, the pre-advance expenditures, and the expense of Secret Service protection.

Michelle Obama's visit to Botswana was a "goodwill mission" to that country. Typically, first ladies take on a highly visible cause to which they dedicate their efforts and bring press attention. Promoting "youth wellness" was among Mrs. Obama's stated goals for her African trip.

Back home, at state dinners and other functions, first ladies rule the roost when it comes to laying out a lavish gourmet spread. Americans have a right to be proud of the superb quality of these occasions. But taxpayers should be aware that they pay dearly for the fact that official White House entertaining has achieved a world-class level of excellence. The grand scale on which personal and official guests are received at the White House, right down to rose-water finger bowls proffered to guests by footmen, is unsurpassed anywhere in the world.

Since President Grant gave the first state dinner in 1879 to honor King Kalakaua of the Sandwich Islands (now Hawaii), state dinner invitations have become the most sought after, and the dinners the most press-worthy, of all the state-sponsored feasts around the globe. In many ways, as a former White House chef put it, "the State Dinner has become more like a Broadway play than a dinner." These events are perfectly choreographed in every detail, from the invitation's arrival to the final course of the meal, and beyond.

A guest receives a keepsake-quality invitation printed on heavy cream colored stock with the details spelled out in elaborate calligraphy. Obviously, refusal of an invitation from the first family is considered the ultimate social blunder. When a woman invited to an Eisenhower state dinner did not arrive, the First Lady expressed her dismay to her social secretary. The social secretary suggested they not be too hasty as the woman may have died—to which the usually mild-mannered Mamie responded, "She better have."

Some presidents have even hosted as many as a dozen or more state dinners a year. With various configurations of traditional rectangular tables and seating arrangements, approximately 100 guests can be fit comfortably into the State Dining Room. Using the round tables Jackie Kennedy first introduced, the room can accommodate as many as 130. The large number of guests and the frequency of events might seem daunting to the homemaker who is challenged by something as simple as entertaining a bridge foursome or putting up relatives at the holidays. But our country's first

Place setting at state dinner in honor of South Korean President Lee Myung-bak and wife Kim Yoon-ok, October, 2011 *(Photo with permission MANDELNGAN/AFP/Getty Images)*

Dining room setting for state dinner in honor of Australian Prime minister John Howard, may 16, 2006   (Photo with permission Shealah Craighead/White House/Getty Images)

lady has more than a little help when she has guests.

Official calligraphers write out invitations, place cards and menus—they are veritable "works of art" (for which many guests concoct the wildest excuses as they slip them into their pockets at the end of the dinners).

The vermeil tableware, which consists of sterling silver silverware dipped in gold, had been purchased by President Monroe in 1817 for the White House after it was burned to the ground by the British and had to be rebuilt and refurbished from the ground up.

The White House china collection is a historical wonder, as well as a connoisseur's dream come true, but not all patterns are available in enough settings to serve full-blown State banquets. Often, first ladies choose their own patterns or use the State Department

Service with its "stars and stripes" border, copied from the original set purchased by First Lady Edith Wilson in 1918. Often the particular china used at a state dinner changes with each course. And at every place, pearl-handled knives and solid silver gold-filled spoons and forks are provided—just like all the other pieces of flatware at each place.

The White House chefs are also some of the most celebrated in their field. Of course, when they leave office, their cookbooks fly off the bookstore shelves! During their time at 1600 Pennsylvania Avenue, at least one of them is on duty at any hour—night or day— to cater to the slightest craving of any member of the presidential family or guests. For the state dinners, they meet the challenge with spectacular dishes, even preparing favorites from the home countries of a dinner's honoree.

As noted previously, a vestige of the White House's thrifty beginnings survives in the fact that first families pay for the food content of their personal meals; even so, the total grocery budget of the White House is staggering. Whether for fancy menus at official dinners or for those more modest occasions when the president or first lady is only feeding the on-site staff, the taxpayers pick up the tab.

For White House state dinners, there is, of course, the matter of deciding on the guest list, approving the menu and choosing the after-dinner entertainment. First ladies generally do involve themselves in this fun component of the whole process. If you haven't been invited to the White House for dinner, you can find solace in the excuse given to a social hopeful by a former first lady: "We want to leave room for natural growth of the list over the years." One can only hope to be included in that organic process!

Almost from the nation's start, dancing has been a part of presidential entertaining. Dolly Madison introduced dancing as part of a typical state dinner, and was the cause of the first First Lady's furor when the dance she introduced was the waltz. Other critics of this then scandalous dance called it "the hugging process set to music." If you find that hard to believe, further evidence of how outrageous the dance was considered is the fact that an early nineteenth century Pope outlawed the dance throughout the city of Rome.

Americans, however, embraced the trend that was so popular with nobles and royalty all through Europe. Other presidential administrations also added dancing, right up to the time of the plain-speaking former general of the Union Army, Ulysses S. Grant, who said about his musical knowledge, "I only know two tunes. One is 'Yankee Doodle' and the other isn't."

Today, if there is dancing at the White House, it usually takes a back seat to performances by the many famous entertainers and musicians whom the President can easily commandeer. After all, there aren't many musicians whose careers wouldn't benefit from being invited to the White House. Stars in any field are eager to perform pro bono at the White House for after-dinner entertainment in exchange for the publicity that comes with such a gig. And musicians invited to state dinners even get some down time: during the reception period before dinner, show tunes and lively music will be played superbly by "the President's Own," the beautifully uniformed members of the historical Marine Concert Band—a group created by an Act of Congress in 1779.

Should the first lady prefer to attend a singer or musician's concert on a night when affairs of state call for a lavish dinner, she can leave all of the details to her experienced specialists. Absent a first lady's involvement, the State Department will determine who sits where, according to the diplomatic ranking of guests; the five-star chefs will plan and prepare the dinner; and the Floral Arranger will set up the centerpieces. The White House staff will then set each place according to tradition, while the Social Office will determine the entertainment for the night. In short, if a first lady wishes to leave all the details to the specialists, all she need do is pick out her dress for the evening—and she even has someone whose job it is to help her into it.

"Michelle Obama told ABC's Barbara Walters that Bo has an enviable life, and she wouldn't mind being reincarnated as the family pet in her next life."

—Olivia Katrandjian, ABC News Blog, December 24, 2011

CHAPTER SEVEN

Even the First Canine Lives Like Royalty

Matched against the many significant and high-value benefits that come with the presidency, something so minor as pet sitting may seem like a matter of little consequence. But devoting a small chapter to this presidential perk serves a significant purpose in our discussion; to me, it is a perfect example of the total care and comfort we provide for a president and his family. Not unlike her beloved corgis that so famously obey every gesture and command of Britain's reigning monarch, Queen Elizabeth, America's First Pet, Bo, a black-and-white Portuguese Water Dog, is a symbol of the President as master of every aspect of his life and his job.

Furthermore, it is another prime example of how, unknowingly, we citizens have accepted responsibility for any presidential whim, no matter how personal, no matter how small. Our willingness to relieve presidential families of responsibility for any chore, even something so basic as cleaning up after a pet, shows how far we have let our presidents become separated from the normal day-to-day lives of the nation's populace.

First families generally have at least one pet. Even if they don't want one, their public relations people often recommend it. Dogs especially give an important touch of warmth to first family photo ops. This also explains why few first families have had cats; it is hard to get a cat to come when called, perform tricks for the cameras, or look like it really cares about its owners. In contrast, dogs are naturally friendly, making for good camera fodder, and almost every first family has had at least one dog, more often two. Some first families have had a kennel-full, insuring that there is always a dog or two on hand for the media to snap pictures of and report about.

John Quincy Adams had a dog—and by the way, he also had a pet alligator that he kept in a bathroom in the East Room. Martin Van Buren had dogs and a pair of tiger cubs. If you want to talk about a patriotic and "republican" stable, James Buchanan had a pair of bald eagles and two elephants! President Harrison's family had dogs but they also had a goat named Old Whiskers. The Hardings had a dog named Laddie Boy and a pet squirrel named Pete. Woodrow Wilson had a ram that liked to chew tobacco. Wilson also kept a herd of sheep on the White House lawn. During WWI, the President kept the sheep in support of the war effort. The sheep cut the lawn by eating the grass, and their wool was auctioned to raise money for the American Red Cross.

President Wilson's sheep on the White House lawn. . *(Photo with permission from the Woodrow Wilson House, Washington DC)*

President Calvin Coolidge's wife, Grace, cuddles a favorite pet, Rebecca , the raccoon
(Reprinted with permission from the Vermont Historical Society)

President Coolidge had a dog named Rob Roy, and First Lady Grace Coolidge had a pet raccoon named Rebecca, which had its own house on the White House grounds and was fed an exotic diet of green shrimp and persimmon.

During the presidency of Franklin Delano Roosevelt every schoolchild could tell you his dog's name was Fala. Caroline Kennedy had dogs, cats, a canary, hamsters, rabbits, and a pony named Macaroni.

When Lyndon Johnson's mutt, Yuki, howled for the camera, LBJ howled along with her. Bill Clinton had a cat named Socks and a golden retriever named Buddy. Barbara Bush wrote a book about her dog Millie, and when Millie had pups, she turned what had been Nancy Reagan's White House hair salon room into a dog nursery. The Obamas added the traditional dog, this one named by Sasha and Malia after Mrs. Obama's father's nickname and the first name of musician Bo Diddley. Bo became the nation's top dog.

Coming off Air Force One at Andrew's Air Force Base, well-rested First Canine Bo Obama makes his way back to White House after family vacation on Martha's Vineyard. *(Photo with permission from AP Photo / Alex Brandon)*

Bo made the news when he and his handler were flown to join the president on vacation in Maine. It has been reported that the first family's dog handler was paid $102,000, last year. One wonders if he also was among the White House employees we were told received a 9% raise.

Are you still wondering why you should care whether a first family chooses to have one presidential pet, or a vast number of pets, during the family's stay at 1600 Pennsylvania Avenue?

Well, consider this: when the photographers are not present and the presidential kids are tired of playing with them, who tends the first families' pets?

If you live in the White House, you don't have to worry about training your pet, feeding your pet, walking your pet, building a house for your pet, entertaining your pet, or cleaning up after your pet. Around the clock, the taxpayers pay for folks to do that for you. That's just another budget item in that long list of totally indulgent first family perks.

"The average American could buy a house for the amount of money it takes to run Air Force One every hour. The U.S. Military has provided an updated estimate on that cost...and the number is staggering–$181,757 per hour."

—Fox News, November 24, 2010

CHAPTER EIGHT

---◆•◆•◆---

BillionAir! Flight Services
Fit for a King

As we have written, Columbine III, the presidential aircraft used during Eisenhower's terms, cost the taxpayers a little under $3 million. Today's Air Force One and its twin, Air Force Two, cost us nearly $650,000,000, an increase just short of twenty two thousand percent! (22,000%)! And that $650 million is just the original cost of the airplanes. It does not include the fuel, maintenance, crews, training and practice runs, accompanying planes, backup or replacement planes and their crews, the hangars, supplies and spare parts, and everything else that goes into making these expensive birds fly smoothly. Also not included in that $650 million price tag is a staff of more than sixty individuals who ready the airplanes for flight, chart their paths, arrange the provisioning, supervise the interior maintenance, and, except for ticketing, handle the myriad tasks of your average commercial airline staff.

A rough estimate of how much all this costs is ready at hand; the annual budget of the United States Air Force includes an additional $200,000,000—that's 200 million!—just for Air Force One operations.

According to our military source, flying Air Force One for one hour, considering the military and civilian in-air and on-ground support, the fuel and maintenance of One plus its tagalong and support aircraft, costs the taxpayers $181,757! $181,757.00 an hour! Remember that the next time Air Force One comes to your town. How many hours was it round-trip from Washington? For political purposes?

Air Force One carrying President Barack Obama lands aboard Marine Corps Air Station, Miramar, CA Sept 2011. Obama flew into Miramar before a presidential campaign stop in La Jolla. *(Photo reprinted with permission from the Department of Defense)*

President Obama waves to guests and service members as he exits Air Force One in Miramar, CA. *(Photo reprinted with permission from the Department of Defense)*

In 1943, President Roosevelt became the first of our presidents to fly while in office. Ten years later, a commercial aircraft entered the same airspace as the airplane carrying President Eisenhower. It was an honest error. Ike's airplane was Air Force 8610, which became confused by air traffic controllers with an Eastern Airline's flight, also numbered 8610. To avoid any future confusion over numbers, the Air Force created a call sign that could not be confused with any other: Air Force One. Actually, now it is two identical Boeing 747s. Air Force One and Air Force Two are identical to one another with only one exception: the tail code on one is 28000; on the other it is 29000. With the exception of that small indication on the tail decal, even the designers at Boeing could not tell them apart. The two planes alternate being designated Air Force One or Two.

Each airplane has a range of 6,800 miles. Additionally, the Air Force is capable of refueling these planes in midair, meaning, in essence, that the range of the president's personal airplane is unlimited. The sun may never have set on the British Empire, but the Emperor of America could keep pace with the sun if he needed or wanted to. The aircraft that are Air Force One and Two also have onboard electronics that are especially treated to protect against being shorted out by an electromagnetic pulse. Each airplane, in addition to the 80 telephones onboard, also offers highly advanced secure communications equipment that allows the aircraft to function as a mobile Command Center. In total, the two Ones are a combination of an ultra-luxury hotel and a super-secret military command post—that can fly.

Operated by the Presidential Airlift Group, which is part of the White House Military Office, each of these truly massive planes is more than 231 feet in length—almost as long as a football field, and double the size of the two presidential planes that were in use just 20 years ago. Those aircraft were also extraordinarily outfitted. While the interior of President Reagan's One was designed by Nancy Reagan in a style reminiscent of the American Southwest with some Formica and plastic coverings, today's Ones are richly finished in burled woods and glove leather. The two planes are the most costly non-military aircraft ever created.

We also have to add the cost of training and salaries for the military personnel involved, and the cost of the supporting cargo aircraft that carries the presidential limousine and cars for the Secret Service—not to mention the escort fighter jets that accompany Air Force One, the supporting ground crews, hanger costs, etc., etc., etc. As usual with government spending, nothing's too good for the office of the president, thanks to the blank checks the taxpayers have unwittingly provided for these purposes.

To say these planes are well-outfitted is a monumental understatement. They have three floors and 4,000 square feet (more than twice the size of the average American home), all outfitted in state-of-the-art, high-flying luxury. The quarters for the president and first lady are bigger than all but the most spacious of luxury condominium units. There is the presidential office, of course, the first family's dining room, and a conference room big enough to hold a meeting of the entire executive cabinet, plus many assistants.

When the president is on board, the specific plane he is on, out of the two identical planes, becomes known as Air Force One. In presidential travels, the second plane follows, in part as a decoy but, more realistically, for quick substitution in case the first should experience difficulty. So when presidents travel, not one but two of these great planes are in the air!

There is a well-stocked pharmacy aboard, as well as a fully equipped operating room, X-ray facilities and, of course, accommodations for the traveling surgeon and members of his medical staff. Three of those aboard Air Force One are qualified projectionists, ready for those moments when the first family wants to watch movies in the air. In case the president should care to exercise, Air Force One also has a fully-equipped gym.

In the back of the plane are office areas for senior staff members, and work and rest areas for presidential staff members and members of the press who might be traveling with the president. The Air Force One crews have their hangout and rest quarters in what would be the first class section on a commercial 747. That area also has one entire walk-in closet designated "For comic book storage." We am serious!

On a typical commercially flown 747-400, there are three pilots in the cockpit, and five other members make up the cabin crew. Those five are there to serve the needs of several hundred passengers. On Air Force One there are not five but twenty-two crew members and, according to National Geographic's website—and it bears repeating—five chefs on duty to serve the first family and those the president invites aboard.

There is not one but two galleys on Air Force One, both of which consist of full-sized kitchens capable of turning out 100 meals for one sitting. There is also refrigerator and storage space to facilitate the serving of up to 900 more meals before landing. With two kitchens and five chefs aboard, the kitchens are manned and ready to serve any request, twenty-four hours a day, while the planes are in use.

For food preferences, to call this first class service is an understatement because it goes far beyond that. Complete records are kept of the preferences not only of the first family but also of dozens, if not hundreds, of key staff members. Does the Chief of Staff like his filet mignon black on the outside, rare in the middle? Does the first lady prefer trout or cold salmon? The chefs on One will know that President Obama likes his hamburgers medium well, with lettuce and tomato, cheddar cheese and Dijon mustard. Oh, yes, and with plenty of hot french fries! The chefs even have a chalkboard on which they keep track of how every person aboard likes his or her coffee: regular or decaf, black or with milk, cream, or half-and-half, with Sweet'n'Low, honey, sugar, corn syrup or Splenda.

Any stingy taxpayer who finds this disconcerting can rest assured that when the president is flying on a family trip, or campaigning, he must pay for his food costs as well as those of his family—though this is not so for the food of everyone else on board. When that gigantic bird is flying on personal business, campaigning for the re-election of the big man or for members of his political party, the first family food costs, as we mentioned earlier, are charged to the president. But what about the food for those five chefs and the twenty-two crew members and anyone else who happens to have been invited aboard, plus the crews and staffs of the backup plane, plus the staffs of the cargo planes carrying the presidential limousine and helicopters for transportation after One reaches the destination city, plus the meals for the extra Secret Service to protect the president away from the White House. What about those added food costs? Yes, indeed, taxpayers do get billed for all those meals.

A crowd greets Obama as he arrives in Cape Cod in August 2011. The President stopped there briefly before continuing on to Martha's Vineyard for a ten-day vacation. *(Photo reprinted with permission from the Department of Defense)*

Unlike other 747s, the twin presidential planes have three entrance stairs so that press and staff travelers can enter without passing through the presidential areas of the plane. It goes without saying that the two planes that alternate as Air Force One are fully outfitted with the world's most advanced air-to-air and air-to-ground satellite communications, plus the most sophisticated security and defense capabilities. And one more thing— the president might well be the only person in U.S. airspace who is allowed to use his cell phone while in flight if he wants to!

In addition to the twin planes that constitute Air Force One and the Wannabe, there are a great many other airplanes waiting to serve the first family. When Mrs. Obama or the children fly without the President, they usually travel in one of the many other jumbo jets that are part of the Presidential Fleet.

First families, unlike ordinary citizens, can set their watches by the scheduled arrivals of their flights. Obviously, it would be embarrassing if Air Force One delivered our chief executive late and kept a diplomatic greeting committee or foreign leader waiting. And it would be an embarrassment to all parties if the president arrived too early to an empty tarmac or an unprepared crowd. Thus Air Force One, in stark contrast to the planes hired by the contenders for the presidency, always takes precedence over the other commercial and private jets at any given airport.

How can Air Force One guarantee on-time arrival, which is a nearly impossible task for commercial airlines? First, because Air Force One never waits for take-off clearance, which is a requisite, and frequently the cause of delays, for commercial and private flights.

When a president decides he is ready to leave his office, he walks 100 yards on the South Lawn to his waiting helicopter, which delivers him to Andrews Air Force Base to board Air Force One.

Whenever the Number One Man decides it is wheels-up time for the Number One Airplane, all other area aircraft are held on the ground or put in holding patterns while One's superb pilots get the air to themselves. One can almost hear the crackling of the radios as various air traffic controllers relay urgent orders to one another to delay all other flights!

Moreover, Air Force One's pilots always build weather-caused delays and later-than-expected departures into their flight schedules. If out-of-control delays do not occur, Air Force One pilots take the great airplane on a time-eating zigzag route to be sure the big bird puts wheels down at precisely the planned moment—no thought given to the cost, let alone the "carbon footprint" that this practice entails.

The Re-election Power of One

Americans feel proud to know that all this floating luxury is at the disposal of our commander in chief. What a great statement of power and authority these airplanes make when they deliver our president to foreign meetings! But what about personal and/or political usage of the planes? In the 365 days of his first year in office, President Obama made 160 trips on Air Force One. Twenty-eight of those trips were for political fundraisers, including seven for campaign rallies. Who pays for the operating costs of Air Force One and the following "Wannabe" as well as the support aircraft carrying the extra security details and the transport of Marine One to take the Chief from the airport to the city, and the transport of the "Beast," the presidential limousine for transit around town? Who pays for the costs of all that equipment, and the staggering costs of fuel and spare parts and ground support and personnel and hangar and maintenance? You do!

A member of the 89th Airlift Wing, responsible for One's maintenance and operation, has pegged the hourly cost of running Air Force One at $181,757; that is $181,757 per hour! Multiplying that by the number of hours round trip to a destination city, it's no wonder the Air Force Budget carries an "Air Force One" budget item of $200,000,000. One would hope that also covers the costs of the dozens of ground support civilians and military in the Presidential Airlift Group, which plots the courses, provisions and maintenance of the two Ones. And then there are the additional costs associated with the advance teams, the military personnel and the costs for their recruitment, training and the provisions for their retirement. Given all these expenses, one could likewise hope that more thought would be given to the usage of this presidential perk when it comes time for the incumbent to run for re-election. Instead, common sense ethics fly out the window when every sitting president takes full advantage of every aspect of the White House and Air Force One to help him get re-elected.

It is hard to overestimate the power of Air Force One for political use in campaigning. In 1975, I visited with former President Nixon in an attempt to persuade him to back Governor Reagan's bid for the presidency. The former president informed me that his preference for our next commander in chief was not incumbent Gerald Ford but rather John Connally, the former Texas governor who had been Nixon's Secretary of the Treasury. When I reminded him that Governor Connally was a Democrat, Nixon replied, "We could work something out. And I like Ron. He has been a good governor. But in any case, there is no way your Ronald Reagan or my John Connally is going to take the nomination away from Gerald Ford. When you can land at your destination on Air Force One, be piped off to 'Hail to the Chief' and speak from a podium that bears the Presidential Seal, it is nearly impossible for anyone to take the nomination away from you." Certainly travel by Air Force One makes a very, very powerful political statement. Little wonder it is used constantly as a campaign tool.

Marine One, a Fleet of Presidential Helicopters

As listed in the 2008 Marine Corps budget, estimates have jumped from $6 billion to more than $11 billion to purchase the on-order addition of the 28 new helicopters we mentioned earlier for Squadron HmX-One, the Presidential Helicopter Fleet, which currently numbers 35 of these whirlybirds.

These are the most well maintained helicopters in the world, requiring perfect performance, big crews, high-level security, and big expense! When a particular helicopter carries the president, it is, for the duration of that trip, designated as Marine One. The most commonly used helicopter for the president is an updated, luxurious version of the SikorskyVH-60N. In all, there are four different models in the Presidential Fleet. Two are cargo helicopters. The others are personnel carriers for support troops, staff or press. The Air Force and the Marine Corps do everything they can to make the presidential trips seamless and smooth.

With a crew of four and very comfortable seating for fourteen passengers, Marine One has some great features. These new 64-foot behemoths, which stand nearly 17 feet tall, are capable of landing far more softly than the average helicopter, thanks to their special energy-absorbing landing gear, meant to help passengers survive a possible crash. These helicopters also have protective armor that can withstand attacks by 23 mm shells, and self-sealing, puncture-resistant fuel tanks to minimize danger of explosions or fires. The newly budgeted presidential helicopters will also have video conferencing and encrypted communications gear to allow the president and his crew to reach advisers, military commanders, foreign leaders, or a campaign's political advisors, instantly and secretly.

For a presidential trip, in addition to the president's helicopter and its Marine One wannabe, there are troop carrier helicopters

Marine One, the presidential helicopter, departs the South Lawn in 1998. *(Photo with permission from AP Photo/Susan Walsh)*

used for staff and press. At the point of destination, the support chopper lands first, then a personnel carrier, followed by the backup presidential helicopter, and then Marine One.

Our Marine Corps advisor estimates the cost of operating Marine One alone at $8,450 an hour. Three to five additional helicopters invariably accompany Marine One. Even if only three were used, rather than all five, the cost to taxpayers would be $25,350 *per hour*. It probably doesn't need to be pointed out that a president racks up a lot of hours on his whirlybird. One might be tempted to point out that trips made on the executive helicopter are much more economic than Air Force One. What you need to take into consideration here is that for all but the shortest of trips, the President generally limits his use of Marine One to its primary use: getting him to and from the air force base so that he can take the roomier, more comfortable and better-outfitted Air Force One wherever he wants to go.

A case in point: when President Obama went to Williamsburg, Virginia, during his first year in office, he took Air Force One. That meant flying via Marine One to Andrews Air Force Base (a trip of about fourteen minutes) and then boarding Air Force One for the flight to Williamsburg. From Andrews to Williamsburg is a distance by highway of 114 miles, hardly enough distance for One to reach altitude. And, of course, all the support aircraft, personnel, etc. also had to make the trip. The cost of all aircraft and military personnel involved was an estimated $284,000.

BillionAir indeed!

"If Mitt Romney, Rick Perry, Herman Cain or any of the other presidential challengers were to embark on a three-day bus trip like the one now underway by President Obama, it would cost their campaigns tens of thousands of dollars. Perhaps more...But not the Obama campaign. The White House declared that Mr. Obama's three-day trip through North Carolina and Virginia are official events and not campaign appearances, even though the two states are known to be political objectives of his re-election bid."

—Mark Knoller, CBSNews.com, October 18, 2011

CHAPTER NINE

Presidential Limo and Royal Tour Bus to Rival a Rock Star's

For more than the first century of our nation's existence, the speed at which presidents traveled was literally determined by horsepower. This kept things relatively egalitarian, since there was little difference between the speeds of carriage horses, no matter how much they cost. Back then the White House stable was a modest frame building on 17th Street West, in Washington, a block and a half from the White House.

All that changed with the advent of the internal combustion engine. Teddy Roosevelt, our rigorous and adventurous "Rough Rider" President, was the first Chief Executive to suggest the acquisition of an automobile for the White House. By the Taft administration, the former horse stables on 17th street were phased out and replaced by a garage, which is one of the largest non-commercial spaces in downtown Washington today. In fact, President Taft was the first U.S. President to use motorcars exclusively, with no reliance whatsoever on horse-drawn transport. Taft set a precedent, but unfortunately failed to establish a lasting tradition in terms of taxpayer expenditures, since he paid for the first presidential limousine from his own funds!

That first presidential motorcar was a 1909 7-passenger White Motor Company Model M, a 40-horsepower, steam-driven behemoth. During Taft's administration, the burgeoning "Presidential Stable" also included a 1908 Baker Motor Company Electric, and a Pierce Arrow Vandellette.

Taft and Mrs. Taft in the 1909 White Steamer they personally purchased. General Motors LLC. *(Photo with permission, GM Media Archives)*

Until the assassination of President John F. Kennedy, most presidents rode in convertibles, all the better to wave to an adoring public. Although three presidents had been assassinated before Kennedy, none were shot while traveling in an open car. Even that first automobile of President Taft's had an open seat for the President and his wife. The Kennedy assassination put an end to presidential convertibles.

It is interesting to note that the first two White House automobiles, the 1908 Baker Electric and the 1909 steam-driven White Motorcar, were comparatively friendly to the environment. Not so today with the monstrous multi-ton, fuel-guzzling presidential limousines!

Few places provide a safer haven for the president than the present presidential "Beast," or, alternately, President Obama's new train-car-sized touring bus. With more steel and durable metals in their armor-plating than some of the tanks our brave servicemen take into battle, these mighty machines are small fortresses. They are built to survive any sort of attack the Secret Service can foresee, and to provide oxygen and life support, if needed, when sealed against attackers.

Franklin D. Roosevelt greeting well-wishers in 1937 General Motors LLC. *(Photo with permission, GM Media Archive)*

President Truman's limousine, circa 1947 General Motors LLC. *(Photo with permission, GM Media Archives)*

Dwight D. ("Ike") Eisenhower, 1953 General Motors LLC. *(Photo with permission, GM Media Archives)*

Ike's topless Cadillac, 1956 General Motors LLC. *(Photo with permission, GM Media Archives)*

A 1983 limo used by President Ronald Reagan General Motors LLC. *(Photo with permission, GM Media Archive)*

As his car, the "Beast," awaits, President Obama thanks well-wishers, supporters and contribtors in San Diego, CA Sept. 26, 2011. *(Photo with permission from the Department of Defense)*

The last attack on a president was on March 30, 1981, when John Hinckley wounded recently elected President Ronald Reagan with a handgun. Fortunately, Hinckley was an erratic marksman. His wild shots hit several other individuals before the sixth and final round he fired finally struck President Reagan in his left underarm, grazed a rib and lodged in his lung, stopping only an inch from his heart. Ironically, the heavy armor plating of the presidential limousine was what caused Reagan to be wounded. Hinckley's last shot had ricocheted off the bullet-resistant car, entered the narrow space be-tween the hinges of the open car door, and hit Reagan in the chest as Secret Service agent Jerry Carr valiantly shoved him into the safety of the limousine.

President Obama's limousine has a body of military-grade armor made of steel, aluminum, titanium and ceramics. Each door, with its 5-inch-thick armor plating, weighs as much as the cabin door of a

Boeing 757. The car weighs nearly ten tons, and in terms of comfortable luxury, communications technology, and security features, is easily comparable to Air Force One as the airplane's road-going equivalent. After all, the "Beast" has its own oxygen supply, night vision cameras, fire control system and tear gas ejection capabilities. It also carries plasma of the President's blood type. Totally impervious to chemical attacks, the interior of the executive compartment is also eerily sealed off from all outside noises.

The cost of this "beast"? Well, that takes guesswork since there are some 25 vehicles in the Presidential Fleet, and the "Beast" has twelve brothers used as both spares and decoys. None of the twelve "Beasts" will have any residual value. Ever since the terrorist attacks of 9/11, the Secret Service has determined that presidential limos must be totally destroyed upon retirement in order to preserve their secrets from well-to-do collectors. Maybe if such a rule had been adopted during Jimmy Carter's administration, that president would not have so casually disposed of the presidential yacht.

Whatever the cost, one or more of the Beasts always travels with the president or is airlifted ahead of him—no matter if his destination is Topeka or Tokyo.

As for the big buses, they are always accompanied by an ever-present backup decoy and substitute twin. Each of these mega-beasts is built like an enormous tank on 18 wheels. Their sides are made of five inches of armor plated metal. Their sleek, black, reflective windows are bulletproof, and only transparent from the inside looking out. The tires cannot be punctured with a bullet. Each bus has its own oxygen supply. It is just the latest addition to the already impressive fleet, bringing even more grandeur and envy to the two-mile-long royal procession that makes up today's campaign-impressive presidential motorcade.

From the street, each of these buses is overwhelming to behold. Inside, it's even more eye-popping; there are dozens of plush seats, a private sleeping room and an office for the president, a dining room, a complete galley and enough communications equipment to reach any person or have any information delivered that the campaigning president should want or need.

President Obama boards his campaign bus directly from Air Force One—reflected in mirrored image on the bus. General Motors LLC. *(Photo with permission, GM Media Archives*

The original cost of each of these buses was staggering—definitely well into the millions—and they are all, like each of the limousines, known by the nickname "the Beast," disassembled down to the last screw by the Secret Service and then reassembled by them to be sure they carry no listening devices or potential threats to the president's safety. Like the presidential limousines, the presidential buses will also be thoroughly disassembled and then destroyed after their time in presidential service in order to assure that their construction details and communications secrets do not fall into the wrong hands. Since the government, unfortunately, doesn't do any-thing efficiently, the cost of decommissioning the mega-beasts will likely exceed the cost of the original construction of these buses by the automotive engineers who first put them together, utilizing the full assembly lines they had at their disposal.

The buses' size and power have necessitated new training courses for the Secret Service members who drive them. Included in this is training to enable the drivers to go backward at full speed, guided by nothing but the rear-view mirrors. If you think Hollywood stuntmen get paid a lot, imagine what it must cost to prepare a Se-cret Service agent for something as blockbuster as gunning a multi-ton, two-story armor-plated bus backwards at full speed!

Although President Obama frequently uses the new buses for campaign purposes, his re-election committee is not required to con-tribute to the costs of their purchase or of their operation. Thus, even when they are used for a president's re-election, the costs are cov-ered by taxpayers. To justify the addition of these new buses to the presidential toy chest, a White House spokesman said that "the President needs the buses to get out in the country and meet with real folks in real places."

The White House spokesman could just as well have stated sim-ply that "the President needs them for campaigning." But first, he might need to make excuses for the fact that these buses created jobs where they were made—in Canada.

"ABC News' Jake Tapper confronts White House press secretary Jay Carney over President Obama's schedule, which has included a lot of traveling. Citing a Wall Street Journal article about the number of times President Obama has traveled to swing-states, Tapper bluntly asks Carney if Obama is 'campaigning on tax- payer dime.' 'President Obama seems to travel to battleground states more so than any other president before him…It looks like the president is campaigning on the taxpayer dime more than any other president has done,' Tapper said at a White House briefing."

—FoxNews.com, November 28, 2011

CHAPTER TEN

---◆·▪·◆---

The Ultimate Presidential Perk: A Taxpayer-Assisted Re-election

The seated president has such a huge advantage over his opponents that it almost seems like an exercise in futility to hold the election. With the trappings of office described in this chapter as well as throughout the book, the taxpayer has unwittingly provided the incumbent with a virtually impossible lock on term two.

The economy is in shambles; the United States stands in danger of becoming a third world country; and a change in administration from the top down seems needed. My goal in writing this book is to provide you with some astounding new information so that you are better equipped to help change our country's future—if you so choose.

If I have done my job competently, you should by now be concerned about the range of excessive perks that exist for a sitting president. In this chapter, we will show you the contrast between the incumbent's challengers and the president's experiences as he campaigns, making full use of the penultimate perk we described in Chapter 8 as "BillionAir!" We are going to show you why Air Force One is the "secret weapon" that can give (or may have already given) Barack Obama the election!

Aside from the president campaigning for a second term, for all others in the race this campaign is probably the most physically draining, mentally wearisome experience to which any citizen of this nation can subject him or herself. For a non-president, campaigns are grueling, mind-and-body-exhausting experiences of numbing proportions and the polar opposite of how the experience shows up for the incumbent.

Let's take a look at how this plays out for aspirants.

First, let me say again that we Americans do want our presidents to be comfortable and safe and impress the rest of the world when they land on foreign soil. We are proud that our commanders in chief can deplane from the world's most advanced aircraft when he arrives at meetings with his foreign counterparts. The leader of the United States is the leader of the free world, and as such deserves the adulation and respect we accord him. We can be proud that our president lives as stress-free as humanly possible and that he has all the proper trappings of his exalted office.

However, there is a sobering side to all the extravagant excesses we have detailed so far. These extravagances have the capacity to prove fatal to our most cherished democratic ideals, and we would be foolish to ignore indicators of an executive process sorely out of balance, as some perks help assure the re-election of the incumbent president to a second term. Today, a challenger pitted against a sitting president finds himself pitifully outmatched while we, as citizens, have failed to raise the hue and cry with our elected officials about the fact that the cards are now unfairly stacked in favor of the incumbent.

When he wrote Democracy in America almost two centuries ago, Alexis de Tocqueville presciently warned that allowing presidents to run for a second term would enable them to use the vast machinery of the State to further their re-election agendas. De Tocqueville believed, and I wholeheartedly agree, that it would be better for the nation if we elected presidents to a limit of one term. We might then see commanders in chief whose every action in their first four years in office would not be weighed against—even devoted to—the imperative of being elected to a second term. Two centuries later, we are dangerously close to the point where we have empowered incumbent presidents with perks that virtually guarantee them a second term in office. Once presidents found they could use the new

Air Force Ones without limit as campaign tools, none has been denied re-election.

As de Tocqueville warned, an incumbent president today has his initial four years to earn the loyalty of his supporters and the three million civil servants who consider him their boss. An incumbent president has four years to appease groups that might otherwise prefer his opponent, since he can spearhead federal bailout funds for financial institutions, banks, and manufacturers. he can appeal to and solidify support from citizens whose priority interests are healthcare, employment, defense, environment or many other specific concerns.

If the national committee of a president's political party has deposited $25,000 and advances payments for costs of events it sponsors in the White House, the president can entertain political activists and campaign contributing groups in the mansion. With political assists of this magnitude and in this ultimate setting, it is easy to see how a candidate for re-election to the presidency can assemble a billion-dollar campaign chest.

With Air Force One, we taxpayers have provided the sitting president with the perfect campaign tool, with the ability to fly him anywhere in a very short window of time and in the ultimate of airborne luxury. Aboard either of the Ones, the president must have to remind himself he is not in the Oval Office. Airborne, he has every advantage, the most current of campaign information, the latest news about the community and audience to which he soon will land, heroically, regally. And his campaign committee will be asked to reimburse his voters only pennies of what the trip will cost them. No wonder, since delivery of the new Ones, that our presidents have chosen to spend a very sizeable part of their lives in the air.

With the Ones at his disposal, it is equally convenient and efficient for the president to be in the air as on the ground. The specific capacity they afford the president—the ability to be practically anywhere with minimal discomfort or inconvenience—has made these airplanes the best of the campaign assists that a sitting president enjoys. With these planes, presidents can dash a little politics into the recipe of every scheduled affair of state meeting or event. And of course every president is well aware of this capacity for "back-door campaigning" well before the primaries begin.

The new Ones have been used far more often for domestic flights than the airplanes of previous presidents. They have made it practical for presidents to "drop in on" their fellow citizens anywhere, anytime—to calculated effect. Ethnic groups settle in concentrated communities with multiple generations of their families and friends, so the ever-campaigning president can reach out to a great number of voters by making symbolic flights to select locations.

Without changing pace, a president running for re-election can continue to use the power of his office to appease the hopes and cater to the wishes of group after group and segment after segment of the country's fractious, varied population, knowing full well that the sum of their parts is the national majority. Unless he is on a for-eign trip, the president and the Ones are touching down several times each week somewhere in America, often with little serious rea-son to do so, other than the fact that the president has his eye on his next election.

An incumbent president becomes the personification of govern-ment largesse when he grants federal relief to regions stricken by floods or hurricanes or tornadoes or blizzards. Is the swollen Mis-sissippi out of control? Are there brush fires in Arizona or California? Is the Midwest beset by tornados? Are Northeast blizzards stranding people on mountaintops? Such situations rain down from heaven like veritable manna for a sitting president seeking re-election.

A president also can use Air Force One for onsite military and federal inspections, all the while posing for photos that evidence his apparently deep concern for this or that issue. A president's on-scene actions are covered fully by the press. The publicity spotlights him and puts his personal fingerprint on the federal dollars allocated to relief measures. It is as if he, himself, is delivering the government gold. The benefits his office affords him in his efforts to get himself re-elected cannot be overstated.

A president running for re-election can always find an issue to show his administration's importance to any audience. When speak-ing to a largely African-American audience, for example, President

Obama alluded to the $1.2 billion government monies awarded black farmers as bringing us "closer to the ideals of freedom and equality that this country was founded on."

A president campaigning for re-election also can select events for his calculated appearance in locations where opinion polls show him lagging, or where endorsement was withheld in his previous election. Every state, county and township produces an occasional hero or heroine, milestone, or event that a sitting president can use as his reason for a regal visitation. What city's Chamber of Commerce would not welcome Air Force One stopping by, with the commander in chief on board, eager to attend the town's annual local event? Moreover, any such appearance automatically gets a nod from the nationwide media, increasing the perception of the president as a hometown kind of fellow.

But the ethics violations that this usage of the Presidential Fleet represents are hugely significant. As taxpayers, we have a right to quarrel with the costs of Air Force One being used for campaign purposes. And our arguments are powerful, as there are significant ethics questions about this usage of the Presidential Fleet.

Well into his campaign for the 2012 Republican nomination, Texas Governor Rick Perry was charged with a campaign ethics violation. The Federal Election Commission found that his campaign committee had failed to report the total cost of the usage of an airplane donated by a supporter. Instead of the total cost, Perry's campaign committee had declared only the cost of the seats used for political purposes. Easy to see how they might conclude that the laws in this democracy apply equally to all its citizens. They were simply using the same standard with which a president is permitted to use the entire fleet of airplanes led by Air Force One. An incumbent president can fly that entire armada to his campaign destination, at a cost to taxpayers of millions of dollars, and merely reimburse government for the price of a first-class commercial ticket for each person deemed aboard "for political purposes."

In the early days, when presidents campaigned in official airplanes, the Democratic or Republican National Committees reimbursed the government for the cost of fuel. But in later administrations, rising fuel costs and the thirsty appetites of bigger jet engines made that too pricey for the seated president. With a seated president holding royal sway over the rules of his own expenditures, a new formula was adopted.

Today, when One is scheduled for political use, a manifest is prepared detailing who will be aboard. There are many individuals, like the presidential physician, his valet, and his senior aides, who are expected to travel with the commander in chief, whether or not the purpose of the trip is political. Others who may be along on the trip for political purposes—and this includes the president himself—are deemed political passengers on this manifest. The total number of "political" passengers then is multiplied by the cost of a single first-class ticket to the destination and return, determined by the average cost of such a ticket aboard a commercial jet of the same size. The federal government is reimbursed for that amount—and only for that amount.

Here is a hypothetical scenario that will help to put this arrangement in readily understandable terms. The price of a first-class round-trip ticket from Washington, D. C. to Honolulu is $5,500. If you assume that nine people plus the president are traveling aboard Air Force One for political purposes on a trip to Honolulu, the president's re-election campaign fund would have to reimburse the government $55,000. At the Air Force One operating cost of $181,757 per hour—as reaffirmed by a member of the Air Force—the 18-hour round trip would cost the taxpayers some $3,268,000.

We know these figures seem impossible, but consider the fact that the Defense Department budget includes $200 million annually just for Air Force One operations. We have to assume that cost includes the fuel, upkeep, maintenance and replacement parts for both One and the Wannabe that tags along.

And, since Air Force One never leaves the ground alone, good accounting also would include the costs of the support airplanes which carry the vehicles and ground support materials and Marine One for use on landing. It properly should include the costs of military air cover to give protection during the flight and the costs of those crews. It also has to cover hanger costs and the dozens of ground-based officers and enlisted personnel and civilians who plan, plot and provision in preparation every time Air Force One is used.

Yes, Air Force One makes a powerful statement, but every single time it is used it also socks a very hefty whopping to the taxpayers. In our hypothetical example (which not infrequently becomes reality) the taxpayers would cover nearly $3,268,000 for use of government equipment (for which it previously had paid for its purchase) yet it would cost the president's re-election committee only $55,000. That's something like a mere .017 percent (less than two one hundredths of one percent) of the total actual cost of operation!

And, most often, the White House finds some official reason for the President's visit to the city hosting the political event, his campaign committee contributes nothing, and the taxpayers are stuck with the total of the enormous costs of his political use of Air Force One and its accompanying air armada.

No reasonable citizen would suggest a president campaigning for re-election should be denied the comforts and perks of Air Force One. Of course, the president must have One's security. Of course, the president must have instant access to other world leaders and American forces abroad through the Ones' superb communications' technology. While a candidate for re-election, he remains the president of the United States and we do want him to have the comforts of the Ones.

However, none of the above paragraph argues against the equity of assessing a more fair price for the Ones' use in political campaigns. For a campaign committee to pay only the equivalent of the price of a first-class ticket by commercial air would be ludicrous under any circumstances. And it is really laughable when a campaign committee boasts it has a billion dollar war chest.

Let's imagine a typical situation in which the incumbent president and the contending challenger both undertake the same campaign trip. Compare the travel costs of the sitting president with those of a competitor for his office when each of them takes the same trip to a destination city. Let's say, for example, that the flight is from Washington, D.C. to the city of New Orleans. Renting a medium-size jet aircraft from Washington to New Orleans will cost the campaign of the opposing candidate around $45,000. The trip would take two hours or more of valuable campaign time.

In contrast, if the president who is running for re-election flies to New Orleans on Air Force One, the flight will take only an hour and forty minutes, thanks to officially-sanctioned clearance and the all-important FCC imperatives that Air Force One commands. Assuming the president and ten others are considered on the manifest to be flying aboard Air Force One "for political purposes," the president's campaign committee will reimburse the United States government $9,790—the cost of ten average-priced first-class tickets from Washington, DC to New Orleans.

To recap, that hypothetical trip would cost the challenger's campaign committee $45,000, while the trip on Air Force One would only cost the president's re-election campaign $9,790—while costing the taxpayers $271,500. When the president is campaigning using one of the two Air Force Ones, the incidental costs, such as maintenance and supplies and spare parts of those aircraft, are covered by tax dollars as well.

What about the per diem costs of all those skilled members of the military who fill positions in those handpicked crews—to say nothing of the chefs and the supplies they need in order to cook for the president and his guests? Who pays for the costs of the second Air Force One flying along to be available in case its brother plane has problems? What about the maintenance and costs of the airplanes and crews that go along to accompany the presidential limousine or Marine One for ground transportation at his destination, plus the extra costs of additional security?

Staggering as these are, the costs don't stop there. Before the president even sets foot out of Washington, D. C., an advance team precedes him to his destination. That means the added costs of government airplanes or, at the very least, the price of tickets on commercial airlines. It means salaries and hotel expenses for the dozens who make up the advance party there to scout out good camera angles for the American flag, ensure that the sound system is adequate, place the presidential seal on the podium and set up the teleprompters, line up the locals who will shake the president's hand, determine who stands where, and take care of a hundred other details of trifling importance, all meticulously scrutinized. Who pays for all these added costs?

Who pays for research assistants to detail the demography of the potential presidential audience, in order to prioritize the points he will make in his local "homespun" speech? Who pays the speech-writers who have composed the president's political comments? And what about the salaries and expenses of those who commit his views to the teleprompter, and the tech crew who travel along to handle the equipment? And what about the extra costs of salaries and transportation of security personnel? Then there is the expense of the president's "ground transportation" via helicopter to and from Air Force One.

In late January, 2012, President Obama took Air Force One (along with the Wannabe and supporting aircraft) to New York City to attend a fundraiser hosted by movie producer Spike Lee. Later, Lee posted this commentary on Twitter, "A great night. I heard we raised 1.6 million dollars from the dinner tonight…Ya-Dig."

What the taxpayers may "dig" is that, with the costs of the Ones and the supporting aircraft, plus the military manpower and the extra Secret Service protection, and the costs to New York State and New York City for extra patrolmen and policemen and added fire details, that presidential fundraiser cost taxpayers a great deal more than the amount pocketed by the Obama campaign. We taxpayers would have been way ahead monetarily had we given the Obama campaign committee the 1.6 million dollars and asked President Obama to stay at home in the safety of the White House.

There is another scenario to consider: What if a president is visiting a city to push the candidacy of a congressman or senator or governor—a campaigning individual whose political views you as a taxpayer don't particularly support? Sorry to tell you, but those costs are still billed to you, a further indication of just how powerful a president is, not just for himself but also for his whole party, thanks to the perks that have been accorded him in office. Or perhaps a president is using one of the taxpayers' $325-million planes and its pilots and crew and the necessary follow-up $325-million plane with its pilots and crew, and the follow-up planes for transport of vehicles and supplies, and the follow-up Marine One, and its own "little Wannabe," in his own campaign for re-election? Let's say you support another candidate for president–should you still have to pay for the electioneering efforts of the incumbent?

It might be going too far to suggest that our presidents' campaign committees should be asked to pay all the expenses of a president's re-election. But it can certainly be argued that those costs are for the benefit of the president's campaigns—for his own re-election!—after which he will continue to benefit from all the taxpayer-paid indulgences of the office, as detailed in these pages.

As matters stand, it is you and I who pay for so much of a sitting president's re-election campaign. And not since Franklin Pierce ran for office in 1852 has an elected president failed to receive his party's nomination for a second term. Sitting presidents, in addition to their many powers of incumbency, also have that biggest of advantages—total freedom from the costs, the petty squabbles, the fundraising challenges, and the drains upon the personal energy that form the difficulties faced by the primary contestant who opposes the incumbent for our nation's preeminent position.

The campaigns of challengers with any dreams of success must start more than a year before their party's nominating convention. The president's campaign, by contrast, can laze along in terms of visibility—even while work is going on furiously behind the scenes right up to his party's pro forma nomination, which usually comes about ninety days before the election. Prior to that event, a president's comfortable executive lifestyle remains unchanged, even though he is heavily in re-election mode and his everyday activities are increasingly formed by the concerns of getting re-elected.

Unlike the challenger, a seated president can be assured that every move and every appearance he makes outside the Oval Office or the White House will be covered by the press. Stop in on a police training center in Chicago? Visit a day care facility in Kentucky or a business class in Arizona? The occasion does not have to be truly newsworthy; anytime the president is within camera range, it's news—usually, national news!

In contrast, the non-presidential candidate, or his campaign committee, must hire staffs and consultants and media experts and pollsters and researchers and speechwriters, while also paying for hotel rooms and giant buses and expensive chartered jet aircraft, not to mention such minor details as placards and bunting, national and local print and broadcast advertising, and the many other costs required by a modern campaign. Also, a non-presidential candidate's campaign advisors compete with local politicians to push and pull him in opposing directions.

Speaking of push and pull, until he is selected as his party's nominee, a candidate is lucky if his campaign can afford one or two security officers, and even they usually serve less to protect him than to wedge a path for him through crowds, which could potentially contain assassins or other would-be attackers. After all, even the brother of a former president, Bobby Kennedy, who was then on the campaign trail, was gunned down in just such a chaotic crowd scene at the height of his campaign's success.

The non-presidential candidate is also under continuous scrutiny by members of the press, who butter their bread by reporting on a challenger's every movement, trying to catch him off guard. He must struggle to be up to speed on every local issue, while being knowledgeable about all issues of national interest and staking out positions that will be conveyed to the public via the traveling press.

The candidate must be knowledgeable not only about changing events at home but also those that take place abroad. He or she must be aware of the actions and comments of his opponents as well as all issues of importance to particular communities, to individual states, and to special interest groups—and somehow still squeeze in time for the stream of information and requests spewing forth from his campaign headquarters, his pollsters, and his managers. The challenger must know the standing of every local politician and must appear excited by the opportunity to shake every outstretched hand, kiss every baby, approve every nutty idea and ride the wave of every fad.

Communications are a challenger's constant headache. The non-presidential candidate is always searching for a secure telephone line, then struggling to hear what is being told him on his cell phone above a cacophony of noises pitched a decibel or two above the point of pain.

For many months, the daily fare of the non-presidential candidate would make a dietician turn pale. He will be called upon to eat a Denver omelet for breakfast, baloney sandwiches and deep-fried catfish for lunch, and Philly cheese-steak sandwiches or hot-dogs for dinner—if that's what's popular with a region's voters.

For the contender, small pleasures understandably loom large— a twenty-minute nap in the seat of a crowded campaign bus, say, or the chance, at the end of a long and arduous day, to stick his fist into a motel room's ice bucket for a few minutes respite from the pain of too many hearty handshakes.

He lives on insufficient sleep in strange motel rooms with rattling, sleep-disturbing air conditioners, lumpy beds and thin walls that barely separate him from noisy next-door neighbors. To save funds, his committee may even forgo the motel room and arrange for him to sleep overnight on the campaign bus—where hopefully he will not have to give interviews to press representatives who may be traveling along with him.

While there still are multiple candidates vying for their party's nomination, each contender struggles to get his position straight on many different issues. In primary races, each would-be candidate competes with all the other hopefuls as he seeks venues where he can express his opinions and get press coverage for his events.

Quite often, the challenger candidates are also governors or members of congress. Thus a contender for the White House simultaneously lives two parallel and equally demanding lives; while he pursues the office of commander in chief he must not be inattentive to the office he currently holds. The presidential-hopeful's campaign is also in constant and unremitting need of funds. He needs media advertisements to heighten awareness of his candidacy, to combat new attacks, to clarify positions, and to attract new segments of voters. Advertising is expensive. Even if the non-presidential candidate is leading in the polls, and even if he has a great many active supporters, fundraising will be his constant chore. Even candidates with good name-recognition and high popularity have frequently found themselves so short on funds that monies raised were raced to the bank so that outstanding checks wouldn't bounce!

The non-presidential candidate is running against a man whose name recognition has become not just total but global, a man who has been the focus of every news outlet for four years, and for whom countless babies born in his term have been named.

Always running against the clock to be somewhere far from where he presently finds himself, the challenger to the president often finds transportation costs to be one of the largest line items in his budget. If his campaign can afford it, he will be flying chartered jets to major locations. More often, though, he will be going by chartered buses that are infinitely less comfortable and infinitely less imposing than the "mega-beasts" that the president can use at no cost to his campaign.

The non-incumbent candidate is competing for contributions with all others running against him for the same party's nomination, while also competing with the president and all of his formidable forces. Those political action committees who support a challenger often feel the need to "take out insurance." This means that they make sure they contribute an equal (or even larger) amount to one or more of his opponents. Most often, that fund-receiving opponent is the president! Why? Because he is already in the powerful position of being able to grant, deny or delay certain executive decisions that may be important to a potential donor. In a culture that has drifted discouragingly close to accepting the all-too-prevalent "what's-in-it-for-me" mindset, presidents have a major advantage with such wealthy donors, even when they belong to the "other" party, because of their tendency to hedge their bets and contribute equally to several competing candidates.

Since Franklin Delano Roosevelt held office (he was re-elected to four terms) only Gerald Ford, Jimmy Carter and George H.W. Bush have failed in their bids for a second term. That is the power of the outrageous perks we have conveyed on our sitting presidents. And, very significantly, since presidents learned to take full campaign advantage of the Air Force Ones for which we taxpayers paid

$640 million, no other incumbent has been defeated.

Since he is the current president, it is not taking unfair aim at Barack Obama to show him as the logical example of a system that, with each new administration, has not only seen presidential perks and privileges skyrocket but has, alarmingly, become even more skewed toward the incumbent. For example, President Obama had been in office only a little more than two years when the committee charged with his re-election announced it would raise nearly a billion dollars. If true, this means that the President's committee will have assembled the largest pre-election war chest in the history of American politics! What's more, the Obama re-election committee would only need to invest those funds at 4% interest to earn an additional $40,000,000 to $60,000,000 before the election. Obviously, President Obama's re-election is of great importance to a great many block interests.

For chairmen of presidential candidates' campaigns, it would be hard to over-dream of the possible ways to use the money if you could have a billion-dollar war chest. In the Obama campaign that translates to funds for a 50,000 square-foot campaign headquarters. It means more than ample funds to profile a nation's voters, to search their Facebook entries for trends and preferences, for lists of contacts and friends, and to match specific government programs with voters' prime interests and concerns. Still, the Obama campaign chairman announced that most of the billion-dollar war chest will be spent on advertising. And why not? Today, for an incumbent president's campaign, we citizens cover most of the costs that will be most challenging for his opponents. As we described earlier, among the 469 "assistant presidents" are speechwriters, researchers and strategists—again, 182 of them are paid between $100,000 and $170,000—and, of course, the best of their high-priced skills will be at the disposal of the campaigning president. Some will move to active positions on his campaign staff. Those who remain at the White House will track his success and continuously monitor how the actions they undertook on his behalf dovetail with the interests of particular audiences in specific geographic areas, organizations or special interest groups.

In his campaign for re-election, President Obama's "czars" will also be a rich resource. Their counsel will ensure that his campaign speeches set the right tone with the right emphasis in various regions of the country and for different sectors of the economy. The President's 43 czars will be his contact points with the leaders of every facet of business, finance, industry, and constituents' interests, and will act as magnets for campaign contributions in those areas and arenas.

It doesn't take an Einstein-level genius to calculate just how overwhelmingly favored a standing president is for re-election. Simply put, his campaign costs him far less while he simultaneously raises far more money. These advantages mean he is far more likely to win than his challengers, no matter how personally wealthy they are. Add to this the fact that political action committees (PACs) give most of their money to the more-likely winners, which in this case is the incumbent president. Consider that this same fellow also has four years to woo his biggest supporters and campaign contributors with, for example, luxurious sleepover privileges in the (taxpayer-supported) White House, and the picture becomes abundantly clear.

If you wholeheartedly support the incumbent, this next point may not resonate with you as much as it would, or should, with someone who does not. The taxes of even those citizens who oppose the incumbent and his party unwittingly pay their share of the costs when the president rewards his past supporters or entices new ones with invitations to White House dinners, invites donors to enjoy movies in the White House theater or to use other facilities of the White House "country club," gives them prime box seating in the Presidential Loge at the Kennedy Center, or takes them along for a fun weekend at Camp David or an exciting flight on Air Force One.

Running for re-election, a president also has a nearly insurmountable advantage in terms of foreign affairs. In his first two years in office President Obama spent 55 days overseas visiting 26 countries, some of them more than once. By the time he finishes his first term, President Obama will have flown one or the other of those two great Air Force Ones to just about every major country in the world. Every trip he has made has been thoroughly covered by the press, while also doubling as an educational crash-course for him—quite an expensive education, and all at the taxpayers' expense. In the meantime, a presidential challenger, when he is being interviewed, need only miss the correct location of one of 192 foreign nations or the correct pronunciation of its leadership during a campaign to be branded as "unprepared" in foreign affairs.

Compared to his exhausted, wrung-out opponent, who will by now have been running for his party's nomination for over a year, a president running for re-election comes to the political ring comparatively fresh and vigorous. Taxpayers, including those who may be backing his opponent for re-election, have paid for his privilege to fly, be bused or be driven by limousine to any destination in effortless luxury.

In transit on Air Force One, the president also can access a full background check on anyone with whom he is about to share a platform. He can even be well informed about that same day's squabble in the city council of his destination city. Likewise, he has immediate access to everything his opponents have said about him and what they have said about one another.

No opposing candidate can even hope to match the up-to-date, detailed information at the immediate disposal of a president running for re-election. His citizens, including those who oppose him, have put at his fingertips the world's most sophisticated information bank, at zero cost to his campaign. That memory bank travels with him as he moves, in the lap of luxury, to every political contest.

He can also be confident that his chief of staff will advise him of every development worthy of presidential attention and comment, so that he'll be fully prepared at his next stop as the cameras roll.

After a few hours campaigning, the presidential-candidate is taken back to Air Force One, where he will eat well and rest well before his next strategic briefing and his next highly-visible event.

All Hail to the Chief...

Let's figuratively watch as Air Force One glides to a stop. The main door to the presidential spaces opens. There is a moment's wait. Like a theatrical entrance (which this actually is) the president has been advised to hang back and allow anticipation to build before he steps into the doorway. Now, well-fed, well-rested and looking like the exalted world figure he is, the president waves to the assembled crowds, beaming as he comes jauntily down the airplane stairway. He gives a smart salute to a military aide and camera lights flash as he directs one last wave to the assembled crowd. Next, he steps into the powerful presidential limousine, emblazoned with the great Presidential Seal. Local motorcycle police then escort his all-attention-gathering motorcade, with its caravan of Secret Service forces, and the "Beast" or the mega-bus, which, along with support vehicles and equipment, has been flown to the destination aboard one of the presidential transport jets.

When the motorcade reaches its destination, the president steps out of the presidential limousine or the very-impressive campaign bus and is immediately greeted by a blinding flash of cameras and swept through the masses by a small army of security personnel. Shaking hands with those who have been selected for the privilege of proximity, he moves to the podium. There, awaiting him on his teleprompter, are remarks that have been crafted carefully for him, noting all the hot-button issues for this locale or audience and recounting all the favorable government programs that he and his party have instituted for its specific benefit during his administration.

After his remarks, the president will meet with a select group of the area's party leaders, political principals and campaign donors before being moved efficiently through the crowd back to his motorcade.

Then, with an impressive wailing of sirens, leaving behind an aura of monarchical power, his motorcade will move off to his overnight residence, which is either the presidential suite of a major hotel, or, more likely, Air Force One. Awaiting him aboard One is the ever-present presidential physician we taxpayers have paid for, should the president-candidate need a throat spray or muscle relaxant. Another of his perks, his $100,000-a-year valet, is aboard to slide tired feet into slippers. So is One's gym attendant, who is on call if the president-candidate covets a shoulder massage.

Perhaps, at that last appearance, some point did not go as well as he had hoped, and this is still bothering the president as he continues his campaign for re-election. Or perhaps some charge by an opponent is still ringing in his ears. Representatives of the world's most influential print and broadcast media have been permitted to fly with him in the aft section of Air Force One. He can flatter select individuals to come up to One's presidential quarters for a chance to clarify a point or hear him freely inject the last word in a topic under debate.

Would he prefer it, one of the taxpayer-provided projectionists can be asked to run a distracting movie to help take his mind off politics and campaigning. Or, better yet, if he would enjoy hearing some great music over One's magnificent surround-sound system that too can be arranged. Then, in the safety and serenity of the world's most luxurious aircraft, the candidate-president can enjoy the meal of his choice excellently prepared by one or more of those five chefs aboard before rejuvenating with a good sleep in his spacious quarters. Isn't it worth considering that we Americans are threatening our democracy by giving such an avalanche of impressive assists to incumbent presidents?

Protecting POTUS

The way an opponent is guarded from any hostile or dangerous situations and the way the president is protected are as different as night and day. Bobby Kennedy, as the challenger, enjoyed nowhere near such high levels of surveillance and security. Perhaps that played a role in his vulnerability, assassinated the night of his Democratic primary win in California over Eugene McCarthy, a U.S. Senator from Minnesota.

The U. S. Secret Service is charged with, and best known for, the task we all consider the most important of the Secret Service's duties: to protect the president's personal safety and insure that he remains immune to breaches of security. But that is only part of what they do. Operating under the Treasury Department, the Secret Service has 125 offices worldwide, employs over 3,000 people, and operates on an annual budget of $1.5 billion—at least, according to what's disclosed to the public. In addition to protecting the president, the Secret Service is charged with investigating violations of laws relating to counterfeiting of obligations and securities, financial crimes such as access device fraud, identity theft, computer fraud, financial institution fraud, and computer-based attacks on our nation's financial, banking and telecommunications systems. These tasks make up the little-known array of this branch's investigative powers. America's "Praetorian Guard" thus has fingers that reach deep into the affairs of the most influential and wealthy individuals and the biggest corporations in our country.

Even such information as we can properly obtain about details and costs of protecting our president in trips abroad is sobering. Imagine our costs when President Bush made a trip to London in 2003. It was deemed that the trip required 904 staffers from Defense, 600 from our armed forces, 250 Secret Service officers, 205 from the White House staff, 103 from the CIA staff, 44 from the staff of the State Department, 30 more from the Cabinet, 18 Senior Advance Office staff and 12 sniffer dogs.

If ever the Secret Service gives a sigh of relief, it is when a president is in the White House. The presidential mansion provides security that is as close to bunker quality as can be provided to the president while still allowing him any semblance of a normal life. But while no president ever has been shot within the White House grounds, occasional breaches of security have occurred.

One evening, when President Roosevelt was working at his desk in the mansion, he suddenly found himself facing a young teenager. The youth was standing there, face-to-face with one of the most powerful and difficult to reach men in the world, all because he had taken his friend up on a dare to walk right on into the White House and see how far he could get toward the Oval Office. The boy's appearance of youthful innocence had seen him safely through several checkpoints, from the outdoor security gate, across the White House grounds, and into and right on through the mansion to the desk of the Big Man himself.

In Eisenhower's first term, a man dressed as a painter and carrying a ladder and equipment related to his ostensible position worked on a good stretch of fence on the street side of the White House's South Lawn. After he had painted a bit, he put his ladder over the fence, painted a bit more, made chatter with the guards, then proceeded to move his gear and begin painting the House itself—he was stopped only when he neared the Oval Office. The man was arrested, but when it was learned that all he wanted to do was paint the words "I Quit" on the Oval Office wall, Ike ordered him released. "Hell," said Eisenhower, "Many days I have wanted to do just that myself."

Of course, the Secret Service bristled with embarrassment, and James Rowley, the head of the Secret Service, hung on his wall a printed excerpt from a work by David Rankin Barbee. It read: "When John Wilkes Booth approached [President Lincoln's box seats in Ford's theatre], he was stopped by the sentry and told that he could not enter. 'I am a Senator,' responded Booth. 'Mr. Lincoln has sent for me. I must see him on important business.' His gentlemanly and genteel appearance deceived the sentinel, who allowed him to pass to the President's box."

While the Secret Service men and women may be a bit more relaxed with the chief executive in the mansion, they are invariably a bundle of nerves whenever the president exits those hallowed and heavily protected 18 acres. Whether campaigning or golfing, the president is never out of sight of Secret Service agents, who may be right by his side, somewhere nearby but out of sight, cached in snipers' positions on rooftops in the general vicinity, or even combing the fairways for would-be attackers. It is important not to discount the political value of this protection.

It is true that the U.S. Secret Service is mandated to provide protection to major presidential and vice presidential candidates and their spouses, but only for the last 120 days of a general presidential election, unless a candidate specifically requests protection and those charged with making that decision deem it necessary. As defined in statute, the term "major presidential and vice presidential candidates" means "Those individuals identified as such by the Secretary of Homeland Security after consultation with an advisory committee consisting of the Speaker of the House of Representatives, the minority leader of the House of Representatives, the majority and minority leaders of the Senate, and one additional member selected by the other members of the committee."

If we all agree that cost of protection is not a frivolity, what does this do to our argument against extremely expensive and, in the majority, highly exorbitant, out-of-control, and in some cases, frivolous presidential perks? There is no contradiction. It is realistic to note that these costs rise enormously when presidents leave the White House fortress to attend social occasions, sporting events, a "date night" or go on vacation or travel in order to campaign for themselves or others.

As we have pointed out in these pages, we have given our commanders in chief the ultimate re-election tool. With nearly a billion-dollar air armada made available to presidents at a miniscule fraction of its value, we citizens have, in addition to the perks imbedded in his daily activities, also given our presidents a formidable, perhaps overwhelming and certain unfair advantage for their re-elections

Taken in the aggregate, isn't it worth considering that we Americans are threatening our democracy by giving such an avalanche of impressive assistance to incumbent presidents, enabling them to perpetuate themselves as the holders of office with such relative ease?

"Never doubt that a small group of thoughtful, committed citizens can change the world. Indeed it's the only thing that ever has."

—Margaret Mead

CHAPTER ELEVEN

A Call to Action

We have almost come to the end of our journey together, and I hope you can now see clearly how the rise in perks has been relentless, with little press notice or public attention. Under each of our recent presidents, the value and numbers of the presidential perks have, in fact, exploded, so much that their share of the budget has now reached staggering proportions.

The growing chief executive perks are intermixed in the budgets of the National Park Service as well as the Interior and Defense Departments, all of whose secretaries answer to the president.

There are also twenty-three separate accounts for unspecified "White House" costs. The best of writers, researchers and historians can only guesstimate, but as I reported before, the total yearly cost of today's presidential perks has climbed to somewhere in the neighborhood of two billion dollars since President Obama took office.

One has to wonder if President Obama is even aware of the cumulative costs of his high life. When he takes Air Force One on a political fundraiser, do the costs to taxpayers even occur to him? On a campaign trip, does he ever consider that the cost to taxpayers of moving One, its tagalong twin, and all the supporting airplanes and equipment may be many, many times more than the money he raises for his own campaign? Did either the President or First Lady consider the extra cost to taxpayers (estimated at several hundreds of thousands of dollars) of their going to family vacation locations in separate airplane caravans, in one case less than two hours apart? Perhaps our recent presidents have accepted the growth of their perks by rationalizing that they are woefully underpaid and, in point of fact, they are. Their $450,000-a-year is a pittance compared to Oprah in broadcast, Madonna in concert, or NFL's Tom Brady in a good year. They are even paid far less than George Washington's salary in today's dollars.

Even with his $50,000 annual expense account, a $100,000 nontaxable travel account and $19,000 for entertainment, and oh yes, that extra $1,000,000 "for the president's unanticipated needs," the President of the United States, the leader of the free world, at $400,000 a year, is still paid less than many CEOs of Fortune 500 companies.

However, we must also factor in that most have had remarkable earnings after their presidencies. Since he left office, former President Bill Clinton has earned over $65 million making speeches. In addition to Clinton, every recent president has also assumed his right to the intellectual property of his years in office and sold his presidential memoirs for many millions. Still, presidents must be well aware that their job is underpaid. That taxpayer bargain may result in a president's belief that he is entitled to every plush perk he can envision.

We make no claim that American presidents turn increasingly greedy, but it can be accepted that election to the office does affect great change. No matter how affluent their previous lifestyles or how high their pre-presidency statuses, election to the presidency must be like winning the greatest of life's lotteries. Kings, Queens, Prime Ministers, and the most powerful of private citizens, all stand when you enter, listen when you opine, record your every word. And for physical comforts or lifestyle enhancements, election to the presidency is like having your own Aladdin's lamp and personal genie. You have only to envision something not already forced upon you and it becomes reality. Understandably, all this becomes heady stuff and must make it easier to convince yourself you are worthy of any perk you can envision.

Whatever the rationale, it is ridiculous that no one in our great government is able to put accurate totals on the whopping presidential expenses. It is also ridiculous that no one in or out of government is charged with overseeing these costs. It is ridiculous that Congress spends so much of its time in budget discussions while no one has focused on the presidential extravagances. And it is almost unbelievable that no president in these tough economic times has offered to reduce his side of the national extravagance by so much as a single dollar!

Traditionally, no one on the White House staff is ever asked to testify before the House or Senate Appropriations Subcommittees on Financial Services and General Government. Few members of those committees even attend sessions dealing with White House expenditures. Only a few curious tourists attend the open discussion. It is no wonder the costs keep escalating!

So here is my call for *our* action:

First, I enlist your support for a constitutional amendment, effective with the election of 2016, limiting our future presidents to a single consecutive term. We can debate the number of years of that term. My personal recommendation would be six; but whatever the length of the term, until we limit our chief executives to a single term we can expect to see the winning of a second term remain a major focus of their first. And we have learned there is no way to keep sitting presidents from assembling and using perks of their office to abet their reelections.

Second, I propose we give three very-heavy responsibilities to a bipartisan group. My candidates for that group, just for starters in order to stimulate thinking, would be such well-reputed men and women as Sandra Day O'Connor, the retired Supreme Court Justice, and former U.S. Senators Dale Miller and Al Simpson. Both of the latter gentlemen, incidentally, declined to run for re-election, in part because they believe Congress has become dysfunctional!

I would ask that starting group to agree on other members selected from present or former governors and members of Congress, from representatives of business, the arts, academia, labor, and from city governments. The responsibilities of the group? Several—and some are of democracy-saving importance.

First, I would have its members recommend a raise for our commanders in chief, setting a fair salary for what constitutes the world's most heady post. We should not leave room for future men or women, when elected to be our leaders, to rationalize that grandiose perks are only fair compensation considering their underpaid status for their lofty roles on the world stage.

Two, until that day when our presidents are limited to a single term of whatever number of years, this group should devise a more realistic, more campaign-competitive pricing formula for the political usage of Air Force One and its accompanying air armada. This will be a challenge. Of course, we want our presidents to be secure, and the demands of the office necessitate our chief executive have access to the most advanced communications equipment. As our leader, our presidents deserve to travel in luxurious comfort.

However, the current reimbursements for campaign-related travel are totally unrealistic and a glaring inequity to competitors for the office. Absent Air Force One, no president would campaign for re-election via a first-class ticket on a commercial airline, the equivalent of which is, today, the only amount a president's campaign committee pays. Non-president competitors for the office cannot meet campaign schedules without the lease of chartered jet aircraft, and that would seem a reasonable minimum charge to the campaign committee of a president competing to retain his office.

In 2011, President Obama used the Air Force One armada to attend 113 political fundraisers. It cost taxpayers millions of dollars an hour to fuel the armada. To have charged his campaign committee only the price of a first-class commercial ticket for his transportation makes no more sense than charging his campaign committee nothing at all. Our proposed committee would need to devise a formula better balancing the official requirements of a president and his political needs.

Third, I would have the group demand daylight on the presidential expenditures and recommend methods of accurate and public accounting.

Fourth, I would ask them to devise a method of respectful control over the presidential perks. Today, only a president's conscience limits his additions to the presidential toy chest or their usage.

With his power over the millions employed by his cabinet departments, and with their combined resources available and responsive to any presidential whim, there is no law or constraint - except public clamor - that could deter a future commander in chief from continuing to abuse his privileges into the billions of dollars.

If, after all you have read and learned here, you are as concerned as I am, please respond to this call to action by telling your friends and associates about the alarming facts you have now learned. Urge your local print and broadcast media to cover this story. Write, wire or call your members of Congress and give them your views.

Without action, there is no one, in or out of government, with the authority or responsibility to tell a president that he is not allowed to add to his toy chest or his campaign war chest, regardless of the cost to taxpayers or its impact on the democracy.

If you find that troublesome, I invite you—no, I urge you—to become part of what is still the most powerful sound in the world—the combined voices of concerned Americans!

An Open Letter to President Obama

May, 2012
The President
The White House
1600 Pennsylvania Avenue
Washington, D.C. 20500

My dear Mr. President:

I suppose the odds of your reading this letter are as slim as your losing your office in the coming election, considering how we citizens have paid for the tools that help you stack the odds against any opponent. But in the admittedly slim possibility you do have this book called to your attention, I will guess your people will try to contest some of the figures we have used.

Let me remind you, Sir, so you can remind them, that in the campaign of 2008 you bragged that, as a Senator, you passed legislation (S. 2590) that would give easy access to track every dollar in the country's budget. I challenge your people, or anyone using the tools of that legislation, to verify the hundreds of millions of dollars the government spends to serve the First Family. I also challenge them to wade through the intricacies of the Defense and Interior Departments' budgets and see if they can come up with any more accurate accounting of the costs of your using Air Force One and the resources of our government to unfair advantage for your re-election.

One more thing, Mr. President, and this one is both an observation and a personal appeal. I have had the privilege of serving four United States presidents and being in the Oval Office many times during the terms of others. One of the things that impressed me in all those times in the Oval Office was the total respect universally given to that center of power. In Eisenhower's time, even his brother, Dr. Milton Eisenhower, when he was in the Oval Office, always called Ike, "Mr. President." Ronald Reagan was a casual-dressing Californian, but whenever he entered the Oval Office, he always put on his jacket. That was a measure of his respect for that historical, hallowed space.

You, Sir, in so many of the Oval Office photos taken by the official White House photography, often appear without a jacket and with your feet on the furniture, even on the magnificent desk, the "Resolute Desk," built from the timbers of the HMS Resolute—a gift from Queen Victoria to President Rutherford B. Hayes.

With all due respect, Sir, I remind you the White House is not your house. Just as with all previous presidents, that magnificent piece of our history is on loan to you from the American people.

A humble suggestion, Mr. President: You should not be putting your feet, shoes and all, on the furniture in the home of any of your constituents. And certainly not in the people's home, the White House.

With full respect for you and with prayers for our country,

Sincerely,

Robert Keith Gray

Hon. Robert Keith Gray
Miami Beach, Fla.

Acknowledgements

This egg has been a long time hatching. I got the idea back in August, 2011 while I was at our family cabin in Estes Park, Colorado and happened upon an old edition of Readers Digest. This one had been saved, I suppose, because it carried Q&A interviews with the two presidential candidates. Since I had served presidents in previous administrations, I was intrigued by this opportunity to match candidate Obama's campaign promises to the record of his first three years in office.

On reading, I noted that Senator Obama promised an open administration, and told his interviewer that he had passed S. 2590, under which a citizen "could find answers to any query about his government's expenditures."

As far back as the Eisenhower Administration, I had observed that whatever a president or his key minions in the White House wanted would instantly appear; its cost is never a consideration. Using Obama's Senate Bill 2590, I tried to put a figure on the cost to taxpayers of the Obama presidency. Just as in past administrations, I found that major costs are buried deep inside the budgets of other departments, largely Defense and the Interior Department's Park Service. Challenged, I determined to ferret them out—which is why I am so very indebted to the ever-expanding group who joined me in my determination to present the facts in this book.

Whenever I was ready to give up, one of my many assistants, but particularly professional research specialists Mary Earley and Susan Strange, along with dogged Robin Miller McGrath and my invaluable and very-determined secretary, Indira Sukhra, would come up with astounding new facts to keep me going. Early on, Linda Cashdan of The Word Process provided much appreciated encouragement.

When I was introduced to Judy Katz of Ghostbooksters.com, I found a truly superb editor and taskmistress, who also doubled as a taxpayer fully outraged at what we were discovering. In addition to her valuable input, Judy introduced me to her skilled colleagues,

Wendy Glavin of Katz Creative, a marketing communications guru, and graphic designer Bruce Jacobson of BYJ Communications, all of whom were most helpful in moving this project along. And when we were finished with final copy, we benefited from the critique of legal expert and good friend Steve Chameides, Esq., of Foley & Lardner.

In so many ways, this final version of the book was a joint effort. It started out with the working title, "I Don't Want to Be President, I Just Want His Tax-Free toys." But the further we investigated the higher the total value and cost of the perks climbed, until it was no longer a figure to be merely amused by. We discovered, to our mutual dismay and even horror, that what we had first referred to as "toys" were, in fact, powerful re-election weapons—largely paid for by the taxpayers.

So I thank you from the bottom of my heart, one and all who joined me on this voyage of discovery. Now we can only hope the book does its job as the wake-up call it is meant to be.

Resources

We are also deeply grateful for the following materials and sources:

Books and Articles:

Carl M. Cannon. "An Exclusive Interview with Barack Obama." Reader's Digest (USA) September 2008, pg. 118-123.

Fogle, Jeanne. Proximity to Power : Neighbors to the Presidents Near Lafayette Square. Washington, D.C.: A Tour de Force Publications, 1999.

Groom, John F. The $1.8 Billion Dollar Man. e-book by London: Attitude Media, 2010

Gross, Martin L. Government Racket 2000 and Beyond. New York: Harper Collins, Publishers, 2001.

Jensen, Amy La Follette. The White House and Its Thirty-Five Families. New York, Toronto, London: McGraw-Hill Book Company, Revised Edition, 1970.

Patterson, Bradley H. To Serve the President: Continuity and Innovation in the White House Staff. Washington D.C.: Brookings Institution Press, 2008.

Plesur, Milton – Quoted in Gilbert, Robert E. The Mortal Presidency: Illness and Anguish in the White House. New York: Fordham University Press, 2nd Edition, 1998.

Walsh, Kenneth. Air Force One: A History of Presidents and their Planes. New York: Hyperion Books, 2004.

Wheeler, Scott and Peter Leitner, Eds. Shadow Government: What Obama Doesn't Want You to Know About His Czars. Dulles, VA: Capitol Media Group, 2010.

Williams, Stephen P. How to Be President: What to Do and Where to Go Once You're in Office. San Francisco: Chronicle Books, 2004.

Internet Sources:

"10 Most Expensive Presidential Perks" by Jane McGrath and Jacob Clifton (http://money.howstuffworks.com/5-presidential-perks.htm)

"487 Days At Camp David For Bush" by Brian Montopoli (www.cbsnews.com/ 8301-503544_162-4728085-503544.html)

"A Brief History of Blair House: World's Most Exclusive Hotel," by M.J. Stephey (www.time.com/time/nation/article/0,8599,1871809,00.html)

Bay Soundings - Restoring a Masterpiece, Trumpy Yacht by Mary Kelley Hoppe (www.baysoundings.com/spring03/trumpy.html)

Billy Graham. "A Spiritual Gift to All" by Nancy Gibbs and Michael Duffy (www.time.com/time/nation/article/0,8599,1627139,00.html)

Canucklehead "Obama bus-ted!" by Geoff Earle, Post Correspondent (www.nypost.com/f/print/news/national/canucklehead/_obama_bus_ted _gyztvw89k5MyKNS4B7Qp7O)

CNN.com Air Force One: "The Flying White House" by CNN's Joe Havely (edition.cnn.com/2003/US/10/22/airforce.one/index.html)

CNN.com Political - Clinton earns $65 Million in speaking fees as a private citizen - Article by Research Director Robert Yoon (politicalticker.blogs.cnn.com/2010/06/29/)

"Dale Haney: White House Groundskeeper Also Bo's Best Friend" by Darlene Superville, AP: (www.huffingtonpost.com/2009/11/03/dale-haney-white-house-gr_n_343540.html)

Examiner - Pets of American history by Cori Solomon (www.examiner.com/pets-in-los-angeles/pets-of-american-history)

History of Camp David, A brief history of the Presidential mountain retreat and its famous guests by David Johnson (www.infoplease.com/spot/camp david1.html)

History.com, This Day in history (www.history.com/this-day-in-history/uss-sequoia-becomes-presidential-yacht)

Horseback riding (aboutcampdavid.blogspot.com/2010/10/horseback-riding.html)

"Incredible Journey: How Obama Became the Most Traveled President His First Two Years in Office" by Demian Brady (www.ntu.org/ntuf/pdf/ntufib-161-incredible-journey.pdf)

MSNBC.com Pool Report by Brian Williams (dailynightly.msnbc.msn.com/_news/2007/07/11/4373457-pool-report)

National First Ladies Library, Biographies (www.firstladies.org/biographies/ firstladies.aspx?biography=2)

National Geographic-Airforce One (a_air_force_one.html quoting National Geo show)

National Museum of The US Air force (nationalmuseum.af.mil/factsheets /factsheet.asp?id=568)

National Museum of The US Air force (www.nationalmuseum.af.mil/factsheets/factsheet.asp?id=568)

National Park Service, History Lessons (www.nps.gov/nr/twhp/wwwlps/lessons/103truman/103facts4.htm)

"Obamas Visit Camp David for the First Time" by Kevin Hechtkopf (www.cbsnews.com/8301-503544_162-4785403-503544.html)

"Seven Ways to Compute the Relative Value of a U.S. Dollar Amount - 1774 to Present" (Calculated in April 2011 using http://measuringworth.com/calculators/uscompare/#)

"The Obamas Find a Church Home — Away from Home" by Amy Sullivan (www.time.com/time/nation/article/0,8599,1907610,00.html)

"The Obamas' new dog: Hey, Bo (Diddley)!" by Stormist (popwatch.ew.com/2009/04/12/barack-obama-do/)

Political Hotsheet- "Obama's First Year: By the Numbers" by Mark Knoller (www.cbsnews.com/8301-503544_162-6119529-50344)

President Washington's salary noted in The National Park Service history section (ww.nps.gov/history/logcabin/htm/gw3/html)

Presidential Pet Museum -White House Pets - Millie & Ranger (www.presidentialpetmuseum.com/Pets/millie.htm)

Presidential Pet Museum -White House Pets - Sheep Grazing on the White House Lawn (www.presidentialpetmuseum.com/Pets/Sheep.htm)

Presidential Pet Museum -White House Pets - Yuki (www.presidentialpetmuseum.com/Pets/Yuki.htm)

Presidential Pet Museum -White House Pets (www.presidentialpetmuseum.com/whitehousepets-4.htm)

Presidential Pet Museum -White House Pets 1953-2009 (www.presidential petmuseum.com/whitehousepets-1.htm)

Presidential Pet Museum -White House Pets Menu 1789-1850 (www.presidentialpetmuseum.com/whitehousepets-4.htm)

Presidential Pet Museum -White House Pets- Old Whiskers (www.presidentialpetmuseum.com/Pets/Old_Whiskers.htm)

Presidential Pet Museum-White House Pets Menu 1889-1953 (www.presidentialpetmuseum.com/whitehousepets-2.htm)

Presidential Pets (1921-1945) All Creatures Great and Small (georgewbush-whitehouse.archives.gov/president/holiday/historicalpets2/02-js.html)

Senator Charles E. Schumer for NY web site Press Release (schumer.senate.gov/record.cfm?id=330983&)

Sequoia Presidential Yacht Group - History (www.sequoiayacht.com/history.htm)

Swimming Pool (aboutcampdavid.blogspot.com/2010/09/swimming-pools.html)

The Dwight D. Eisenhower Presidential Library & Museum (www.eisenhowerarchives.com)

The Guardian, "The best perk in the White House" by Julian Borger (www.guardian.co.uk/film/2004/jun/04/1)

The Office of Management & Budget (www.whitehouse.gov/omb)

The Official Web Site of the US Air Force (www.af.mil/information/factsheets/factsheet.asp?id=131)

"The Presidency: Splendid Misery" Monday, July 27, 1959 (www.time.com/time/magazine/article/0,9171,864726,00.html)

"The Right Recipe for a White House State Dinner" By Feifi Sun (www.time.com/time/politics/article/0,8599,2043191,00.html)

The Truman Library (www.trumanlibrary.org)

The White House - Rooms (www.whitehouse.gov/about/history/rooms)

The White House Historical Association (www.whha.org/index.htm)

The White House Historical Association- (www.whitehousehistory.org/whha_history/history_facts-06.html)

The White House Historical Associations, First Kids (www.whitehousehistory.org/whha_classroom/classroom_4-8-firstkids.html)

The White House Museum - Beauty Salon (www.whitehousemuseum.org/floor2/beauty-salon.htm0

The White House Museum - China Collection (www.whitehousemuseum.org/furnishings/china.htm)

The White House Museum Virtual Tour (www.whitehousemuseum.org/index/htm)

The White House Museum, Bowling Alley (www.whitehousemuseum.org/floor0/bowling-alley.htm)

The White House Museum, Family Theatre (www.whitehousemuseum.org/east-wing/theater.htm

The White House Museum, Renovations (www.whitehousemuseum.org/special/renovation-1948.htm)

The White House Museum, Sun Room (www.whitehousemuseum.org/floor3/sun-room.htm)

The White House Museum, White House Grounds (www.whitehousemuseum.org/grounds.htm)

The White House, Annual Report to Congress on White House Staff 2010 (http://www.whitehouse.gov/briefing-room/disclosures/annual-records/2010)

The White House, Glimpse of Presidents (clinton4.nara.gov/WH/glimpse/presidents/html/rn37.html)

TheWhiteHouse.gov -Airforce One (www.whitehouse.gov/about/air-force-one)

TheWhiteHouse.gov -History (www.whitehouse.gov/about/history)

TheWhiteHouse.gov -Tours (whitehouse.gov1.info/visit/tour.html)

ThinkQuest.org - American Presidents- First Pets (library.thinkquest.org/08aug/01450/pets.html)

Trampoline (aboutcampdavid.blogspot.com/2010/09/trampoline.html)

Treasurydirect.gov-Public Debt Reports (www.treasurydirect.gov/govt/reports/pd/histdebt/histdebt_histo1.htm)

Wedding (aboutcampdavid.blogspot.com/2011/01/camp-david-wedding.html)

Wikipedia USS Sequoia (presidential yacht) (http://en.wikipedia.org/wiki/USS_Sequoia_(presidential_yacht)

"Wombats and Such: Calvin and Grace Coolidge and their Pets" by David Pietrusza (www.davidpietrusza.com/coolidge-pets.html)

WUSA9News.com – "First Lady Replants White House Vegetable Garden" by Heather Case (www.wusa9.com/news/local/story.aspx?storyid=99399)

About the Author

Hon. Robert Keith ("Bob") Gray is a Republican activist and public relations executive who has worked in the White House under U.S. Presidents Eisenhower, Nixon, and Reagan and formed close ties to President Bush Sr. He served as Appointments Secretary to President Dwight Eisenhower and later as a member of his cabinet. In the 1960s and 1970s, he served as Washington operative for Hill & Knowlton, a global public relations company. In those years, according to a case study by the Harvard Business School, H&K's clients produced nearly 10% of the GNP.

In 1967, Gray joined the 50-person committee responsible for charting Richard Nixon's path to the White House. In 1980, after serving as deputy director of the Reagan-Bush presidential campaign, Gray became Reagan's first appointment as president when he was named Co-Chairman of Ronald Reagan's Presidential Inauguration.

In 1981, Gray started his own firm, Gray and Company. When he took the firm public in 1985, it became the first public relations-public affairs firm to be listed on the New York Stock Exchange. Three years later, he sold majority interest in the firm to Hill & Knowlton and became H&K's Worldwide Chairman.

In 1988, as one of his last acts as president, Ronald Reagan flew to Gray's hometown, Hastings, Nebraska, to dedicate a communications center Gray had given to Hastings College in honor of his parents.

Gray's book, 18 Acres Under Glass, was published by Doubleday in the United States and by Macmillan overseas. With tales of the visits with kings and queens, to the extended hours spent with the chief executives, the book gives the reader an inner look at the functions and sometimes dysfunctions of Washington.

Gray has been featured in cover stories in Time magazine and U.S. News & World Report, named "Marketer of the Year" by Ad Week magazine, and was the subject of a fifteen-minute Monitor program on NBC. He has received Italy's highest civilian decoration,

Grande Ufficiale.

Bob Gray holds a Harvard University MBA and four honorary doctorates (from Creighton University, Barry University, Marymount University and Hastings College). His current company is Gray and Co 2, where he serves as a consultant to international companies and on corporate boards. Vital and engaged in his 80s, Bob Gray continues to travel the world for business and pleasure. He lives in Miami Beach, Florida.

His website is www.robertkeithgray.com